Democracy and Intolerance:

Christian School Curricula, School Choice, and Public Policy

FRANCES R.A. PATERSON

PHI DELTA KAPPA
EDUCATIONAL FOUNDATION
Bloomington, Indiana
U.S.A.

Cover design by
Victoria Voelker

Phi Delta Kappa Educational Foundation
408 North Union Street
Post Office Box 789
Bloomington, IN 47402-0789
U.S.A.

Library of Congress Control Number 2002114301
ISBN 0-87367-842-7
Copyright © 2003 by Frances R.A. Paterson

For my father, Robert L. Paterson

TABLE OF CONTENTS

INTRODUCTION

When I began this study of Christian school textbooks, I thought of it as a natural outgrowth of my work on religiously based challenges to public school curricula and instructional materials. Having examined what religious-political conservatives criticized about public school curricula, I turned my attention to the nature of the education they considered suitable to replace it. I use the word *replace* in both a personal and a broader, more universal sense: personal because many religious-political conservatives choose Christian schools for their own children, and universal because many of the programs and policies advocated by religious-political conservatives would probably increase enrollments in Christian schools and result in a greater proportion of American education taking place in such schools.

Like many others who observe the public discourse on political issues, I have noticed in recent years a lack of civility and increased, ideologically driven stridency. Our elected leaders appear much less able to compromise and to eschew partisanship than in the past. I was intrigued by what I learned from Alan Peshkin's *God's Choice: The Total World of a Fundamentalist Christian School*, Susan Rose's *Keeping Them Out of the Hands of Satan: Evangelical Schooling in America*, and Paul Parsons' *Inside America's Christian Schools*. That reading and the impressions gained during my own visit to a Christian school in Oklahoma, together with statistics indicating the substantial growth in Christian schools in the 1980s and 1990s, caused me to wonder if some of this sociopolitical polarization might be attributed to a larger proportion of the electorate being educated with Christian school curricula. However, mere correlation does not prove causation. Many other factors during these two decades also have affected the nature of public debate over a variety of social, economic, and political issues. These factors include the rise of conservative radio programming, the increased influence of conservative advocacy organizations (for example, Pat Robertson's Christian Coalition and James Dobson's Focus on the Family), grassroots organizing by conservative organizations, and the funding of conservative foundations and think tanks. It is beyond the scope of this book to argue that the increased number of students enrolled in schools that base their curricula on ideologically driven textbooks have contributed to greater political polarization in the country as a whole, but it does not stretch credulity to conjecture that the education of an increasing number of individuals whose schooling rests on ideologically based curricula may well be *one* factor in this increased divisiveness.

Interestingly, writing about the content of Christian school textbooks required me to adopt both a sociological perspective and a methodology often used by conservatives themselves, especially those whose activities formed the focus of my previous work. With regard to the sociological position, it is necessary to remember that, when looking at the media and popular culture, social conservatives place great emphasis on the pernicious influence on young people of exposure to depictions of "antisocial" or "undesirable" values. If this is so, then exposure to textbooks whose values are inimical to tolerance and respect for others in our society must be presumed to have similar negative consequences. Either what children are exposed to affects them or it doesn't, but one cannot argue logically that sex and violence in popular culture affect children and then argue that bigotry and intolerance in textbooks do not. Liberals don't get off the hook, though, because one cannot argue that bigotry and intolerance in textbooks affect young people but sex and violence in movies, popular music, and video games do not. One simply cannot have it both ways, and so I have attempted to steer a reasonably balanced course in this study.

With regard to methodology, many commentators and scholars who have addressed the issue of censorship of public school materials, especially school library books, have deplored the challengers' practice of selectively quoting from the objectionable texts and accuse the protesters of failing to examine the book or textbook series in its entirety. Indeed, I came close to making that argument myself when I pointed out that the plaintiffs in the two major court cases over the issue of occult content in an elementary school reading series objected to only a tiny fraction of the more than 10,000 stories, selections, and poems in the series. Nevertheless, it is impossible to portray controversial material in a book without using quotations. If an author merely describes the material in his or her own words, then the reader might surmise, rightly or wrongly, that the author's own bias has colored his or her analysis. Therefore, in this volume I have quoted, sometimes at length, from the textbooks I examined so that the reader can draw his or her own conclusions about the worldview they present.

I encourage readers to obtain copies to examine for themselves of A Beka and Bob Jones University Press textbooks and School of Tomorrow/Accelerated Christian Education materials. These books are readily available. By visiting the publishers' websites (http://www.abeka.com, http://bjup.com, and http://www.school oftomorrow.com, respectively), readers can browse their offerings and order online. Actually examining the books leads to a curiously contradictory experience. On the one hand, there is an overwhelming amount of noncontroversial material: Shakespeare's sonnets, the geography of Africa, the electoral college, battles of the World Wars, rivers in Australia, the climate of Switzerland, kings and queens of England, the process by which a bill becomes a law, and so forth. But there also is a sense of disconnection when the reader sees at first glance what looks like a traditional textbook with innocuous illustrations, boldfaced subtitles, and review questions but, on closer reading, finds text that is highly partisan or contains conservative religious-political commentary. Sometimes, the factual material continues without interruption for several pages. But just as often it is laced with editorial commentary, ranging from the occasional sentence to a paragraph or more. In other places, virtually every line of text is opinion.

In Chapters One through Five, I examine the nature of this editorial commentary. Most of the commentary can be described as laying out conservative political and religious positions on a wide variety of social, political, and economic issues. Some of it might be characterized as extremist. The writers' purpose is clear: to persuade the students using these textbooks and related materials that the point of view their authors present is the right one and that holding a contrary position is "wrong" or even "sinful." This is the position conservative religious-political elites maintain vis-à-vis elements of public school curricula that are contrary to their values.

I recognized early on that issues of censorship and challenges to reading materials in public schools interested me because of my background as a public school librarian and the enormous role that libraries have had in my own life. When I was a small child, my father often would take me to a public library, first in New York City and later in Charlotte, North Carolina. I came to love books and the unfettered access to ideas. As I remarked earlier, this book also complements my prior research on religious-political conservative challenges to children's reading materials and public school curricula generally. As I worked on this book and reflected on the larger picture, I also came to another realization. Without intending to, I had immersed myself in a project that reflected another, albeit minor, part of my childhood. Even before I started first grade, my father taught me to say the word *antidisestablishmentarianism*, much to his and my mother's amusement. I remember being told (and responding with considerable pride in my accomplishment) that it was the longest word in the English language. This is almost surely not true now and probably was not true at the time because some scientific terms may well be longer. Nevertheless, I knew the word itself from an early age and its meaning sometime later in my childhood. It strikes me as more than a little ironic to find my research as an academic is tied to issues that flow from the disestablishment of the church in postrevolutionary America to a modern permutation of this phenomenon, the movement to "disestablish" public education.

As I argue in Chapter One, the disestablishment of the church with the development of the common school movement meant, in a very real sense, that church schools lost their hegemony over curricular content. But even though religious authorities lost the ability to inculcate children in denominational theology, they were able to reach a compromise with proponents of the common school under which the public schools would incorporate a pan-Protestant worldview in the curriculum. Of course, I am over-simplifying the profound social, educational, and demographic changes of the last century and a half. But I would argue that this basic compromise lasted until about forty years ago. During the past four decades, an increasingly secular culture and an increasingly racially and religiously diverse population have displaced this pan-Protestant hegemony. The resulting secularization of the public schools, therefore, combined with these other factors, has stimulated the rise of Christian schools and home schooling based on conservative religious and political views.

Christian schools of various types, taken collectively, are a growing force in American education. In some ways, the emergence of these conservative, religious-political education alternatives mirrors the 19th century rise of the common school and diminished influence of church schools. In our own time, it is public schools that are in danger of being disestablished.

* * *

I wish to thank Heather Walker and Jennifer Spreng for their able assistance in preparing this manuscript.

CHAPTER ONE

Disestablishmentarianism for the 21st Century

From days of Horace Mann through the Scopes trial and the 1940 burning of Harold Rugg's history textbooks to recent calls for the removal of J.K. Rowling's Harry Potter books, control of what should be taught to the nation's children has been the subject of controversy. Both Mead and Fraser see the loss of religious hegemony over education as a byproduct of the disestablishment of state churches during the late 18th and early 19th centuries.[1] During the mid-19th century, the common schools with a generic pan-Protestantism advocated by Horace Mann replaced the church schools of the colonial and postrevolutionary period. In response to Protestant domination of the public schools of the 19th century, Roman Catholics established their own elementary and secondary education system. In the second half of the 20th century, conservative Protestants found the public schools hostile to their worldview. Like the Catholics of the 19th century, conservative Protestants faced a well-entrenched, publicly financed system that contradicted the most fundamental values they wanted their children to learn. For today's conservative Protestant parents, the public schools undermine their ability to pass on deeply held religious, social, and, in many cases, political values to their children. But unlike the Roman Catholic Church of the 19th century, conservative Protestants of the late 20th century rightly understood that the increasingly secular public schools represented a loss of hegemony.[2] The frustration of Roman Catholics and the Roman Catholic Church over public financing of a system of education that inculcated their children in pan-Protestantism did not involve a loss of domination, because the Church did not exercise control over the school curricula of the colonial and postrevolutionary period.

In addition, the Roman Catholics of the 19th century, while they viewed public education as inimical to the religious upbringing of their own children, did not view common and public schools of the 19th and 20th centuries as inherently destructive to the nation as a whole. During the last 30 years, however, conservative Protestants have regarded public education as a battleground for the soul of America. As Hunter notes, the current cultural conflict over public education is "all but a formal declaration of war over the public schools" that "conceals a deeper issue — the issue of who controls the mechanisms of cultural reproduction."[3] Because the "schools are the primary institutional means of reproducing community and national identity," the battles over control of education are fraught with passion and fought with unwavering intensity.[4]

Little wonder, then, that using such militaristic phrases as "holy war" and "mortal jeopardy," religious-political conservatives have become increasingly vociferous in their criticisms of the nation's public schools. This criticism has manifested itself in two interrelated phenomena: first, criticism of and challenges to the public schools and public school curricula and, second, a call to convert an increasing proportion of American education to private, sectarian institutions and home schooling.

Conservative Criticisms of Public Education

Contemporary conservatives, especially religious-political conservatives, have long argued that public education is failing the nation.[5] Early religious-political conservative critics of public education include Barbara Morris, Tim La Haye, Mel and Norma Gabler, and Jerry Falwell. These writers portray modern American education as both reflecting and contributing to the nation's social, moral, and spiritual decay.[6]

While Falwell and Pat Robertson disagree on theological issues, they are consistent in their criticism of public education. Decrying American students' lack of academic achievement, Robertson states that "[humanist] educators do not believe reading, math, history, and geography skills are important"; rather, they seek "the sociological and behavioral indoctrination of our children."[7] John Dewey and the "radical leftist N.E.A." (National Educational Association), "an educational establishment run by wise fools," have been responsible for the "dumbing of America" and "the hopelessness and despair" of urban youth who face "a short and unhappy existence."[8] Many other religious-political conservative leaders — for example, James Dobson of Focus on the Family, Phyllis Schlafly of Eagle Forum, Beverly LaHaye of Concerned Women of America, and Robert Simonds of Citizens for Excellence in Education — join the position of Falwell and Robertson. These commentators maintain that public education is inimical to the nation's well-being and its moral and spiritual health.

In general, these criticisms have centered on both the aims and the content of school curricula, and the focus has been on the conflict between traditional and progressive approaches to what schools teach and how they teach it.[9] Among organizational and curricular issues that have generated controversy are cooperative learning, critical thinking, experimental or innovative programs, global education, master learning, outcome-based education, self-esteem programs, shared decision-making, learner-centered instruction, decision-making skills programs, and whole language.[10] Much of the criticism has focused on the content of public school curricula that religious-political conservatives find objectionable. As Hunter observes, "Humans simply cannot tolerate the desecration of that which is most cherished."[11] In addition to extensive studies of the historical and ongoing battle over evolution and creationism, Provenzo describes disputes over humanism in school library books and curricula, most notably an experimental social studies curriculum, "Man: A Course of Study"; "death education"; and values clarification.[12] Gaddy,

Hall, and Marzano document the rising criticism of public school curricula related to the alleged presence of New Age religious material, as well as objections to multiculturalism and whole language instruction.[13] In my previous work, I found that religious challenges to public school curricula tend to cluster around four issues: evolution/creationism, denigration of religion, secular humanism, and occult content.[14] In tandem with their criticisms of the public schools, Religious Right leaders praise home schooling and Christian schools as options for disaffected parents and have urged conservative Protestant families to choose these alternatives to what they frequently refer to as "government schools." At the deepest level, the struggle for control of the curricula taught to the nation's children by the formation of a system of alternative schooling is an effort to disestablish public education.[15] As Jerry Falwell opined in a often-repeated remark: "I hope I live to see the day, when, as in the early days of our country, we won't have any public schools. The churches will have taken them over again and Christians will be running them. What a happy day that will be!"[16]

The schools that conservative Protestants have established to serve their families are a fast-growing segment of the American education system.[17] And, like the Roman Catholics of the 19th century, religious-political conservatives of the 1990s have increasingly sought public funding for this parallel education system through a variety of means. In recent years, many advocates of school choice have been successful in devising programs designed to encourage the privatization of American education. Such efforts include public-to-private school vouchers, tax relief for private school tuition, and private school scholarship programs. School voucher programs may include religious schools from the outset (Florida) or add religious schools once the program is established (Milwaukee). Private scholarship programs, not typically facing legal challenges, routinely include religious schools.[18] Although true public vouchers for sectarian schooling currently exist only in Milwaukee, Cleveland, and most recently Florida, efforts to privatize American education will continue and may accelerate, given the Supreme Court's 2002 decision in *Zelman* v. *Simmons-Harris*, in which the Court held that the use of publicly funded vouchers at religious schools does not violate the Establishment Clause.[19] These programs, whether they are public-to-sectarian school voucher programs, private scholarship programs, or tax-advantaged tuition savings accounts, will enhance the ability of students to attend sectarian schools at reduced or no cost and may lead to increased numbers of students attending such schools, the creation of additional sectarian schools, or both. For these reasons, and because these schools would receive direct or indirect taxpayer subsidization, a closer examination of what many sectarian schools teach their students is appropriate.

Discussions of vouchers, precollegiate tuition tax relief, or private scholarship programs, whether carried on by scholars or other commentators, have focused almost exclusively on issues related to the constitutionality of these programs, their efficacy in terms of student achievement, their effect on public education, their potential to stratify or resegregate American education, or some combination of these issues.[20] What has been conspicuously absent from the current debate about vouchers and other programs encouraging privatization is any discussion of the curricula of nonpublic schools. With the exception of a full-length study in 1993, sponsored by the anti-voucher advocacy organization, Americans for Religious Liberty, and a 1987 article discussing history materials published or distributed by School of Tomorrow, the issue of what students are taught has not played a major part of the public and scholarly discussions of privatization.[21] Some of the amicus curiae briefs filed in *Jackson* v. *Benson* argued that the schools were pervasively sectarian and that allowing students to opt out of religious instruction, as provided by Wisconsin law, was inadequate to protect students from forced exposure to religious dogma.[22] However, the authors of the briefs did not look beyond the mission statements of some of the sectarian schools participating in the program.

Two amicus curiae briefs submitted to the U.S. Supreme Court in support of the respondents in *Zelman* addressed the issues of religious content that is inextricable and pervasive in the curricula of sectarian schools generally, and the potential for excessive entanglement when the government is called on to determine whether a religious school taught "hatred of any person or group on the basis of race, ethnicity, national origin, or religion" and thus should be prohibited from participating in the program as required under Ohio law.[23] It appeared that the arguments of the *amici* may have resonated with both Justices Souter and Breyer, whose dissents repeated many points raised in the briefs.[24]

While the curriculum in parochial schools is similar in many respects to that of public schools, the curricula of many evangelical and fundamentalist Christian schools differs substantially from that used in parochial schools, other sectarian schools, secular private schools, and public precollegiate institutions. During the 1980s, three authors examined the culture of Christian schools, including their curricula; however, their discussions of the curricula of these schools is either scattered or brief, and their consideration of this subject was not tied to the voucher movement of the 1990s.[25]

A relatively easy way to learn what children are taught is to examine the textbooks they use. Curriculum and instruction scholars have long lamented that school curriculum is, to a large extent, textbook-driven.[26] Textbook dependency is even more pronounced in Christian schools with their emphasis on teacher-centered learning, structure, and discouragement of curricular innovation. Indeed, disagreement with and distaste for instructional innovation and a return to the "basics" are part the *raison d'etre* of the Christian school movement and the involvement of the Christian right in school voucher programs and privatization efforts generally.

Although it is difficult to obtain sales figures from either secular or religious publishers, many Christian schools purchase textbooks and curricular materials from three publishers: A Beka Books, School of Tomorrow/Accelerated Christian Education (ACE), and Bob Jones University Press.[27] A Beka appears to be the largest publisher of materials used in conservative Christian schools. When contacted, a spokesperson for A Beka Books stated that approximately 9,000 schools purchase textbooks from the company.[28]

In areas where Roman Catholics are a smaller percentage of the population, it is reasonable to assume that more schools using the textbooks described in this book would receive public funds or benefit from tax relief proposals than in the Milwaukee and Cleveland programs. For example, I found that in a private scholarship program in the Orlando, Florida, area, 52% (n = 24) of the 46 responding private schools used A Beka textbooks, 24% used Bob Jones textbooks, and 15% used ACE materials.[29] In Pinellas County, Florida, 75% (n = 15) of 20 responding schools used A Beka textbooks, while 20% (n = 4) used Bob Jones and 20% used ACE materials. Of these, two schools used both the ACE curriculum and A Beka texts, and three schools used both A Beka and Bob Jones University Press textbooks.[30] In a survey of private schools in southwestern Georgia, 53% (n = 17) of the 31 responding schools used A Beka textbooks and 29% used both A Beka and Bob Jones University Press textbooks. A Beka books also are widely used by home-schooling families.[31]

School of Tomorrow/Accelerated Christian Education materials, which consist of self-instruction booklets, also are widely used in Christian schools.[32] The booklets are 30 to 40 pages long, including review questions integrated into the text and pages with test questions bound into the center of the booklet. The font is noticeably larger and the lines of text more widely spaced than in typical textbooks. A single subject at an individual grade level is covered in 12 booklets. According to Fleming and Hunt, by 1987 School of Tomorrow/Accelerated Christian Education (ACE) materials were being used in 5,000 schools.[33] Students in ACE schools, working alone and sitting in individual carrels, read the material in the booklets and answer the review and test questions. Teachers are not employed in ACE institutions. A monitor maintains order, performs custodial duties, and checks the students' work.

General Characteristics of Christian School Textbooks

Christian school textbooks differ from the materials used in public and other nonpublic and religious schools in several ways. Textbooks published for the Christian school market have the following distinctive general characteristics:

- Absence of gender-inclusive language.
- Explicitly didactic passages in both elementary and secondary textbooks.
- Integration of religious and nonreligious material.
- Juxtaposition of persuasive and factual material.
- Frequent use of identifying descriptors for people, groups, and movements, often implying that some are acceptable and some are not.
- Inclusion and exclusion or noticeably disparate amounts of coverage of individuals and groups, with favorable treatment of some and neutral or explicitly negative treatment of others.

Without noticeable exception, the texts use "man" generically to refer to all people and the pronoun "he" to refer to both males and females. Women are to adhere to traditional roles. The following passage, taken from a School of Tomorrow/Accelerated Christian Education booklet for fifth-graders, illustrates both how the texts integrate religious material into their discussions (in this case, a general discussion of Native American culture) and how they emphasize the importance of female subservience: "The woman of the Iroquois family was the head of the household. The Iroquois did not know what the Bible teaches about the family. 'For the husband is the head of the wife, even as Christ is the head of the church: . . .' (Ephesians 5:23)."[34] Women who embrace traditional roles are praised; women in nontraditional roles, with the exception of such conservative activists as Phyllis Schlafly, are ignored or criticized. Overall, women's suffrage is treated neutrally or in coolly approving fashion, as the saying goes, "condemned with faint praise." That praise is very faint indeed.

Contemporary feminism, especially the Equal Rights Amendment, is roundly criticized.

Conservative Protestant religiosity is pervasive throughout the textbooks, and no study of Christian school textbooks would be complete without an acknowledgment of this characteristic. It occurs in places where it might be expected. For example, all world history texts begin their materials on the ancient world with the Biblical account of creation and use the Biblical account of the ancient Near East as a historically factual account. But religion also appears where its inclusion is unexpected. For example, the chapter on African geography of A Beka's fifth-grade world geography and history book begins, "African history began shortly after the Flood when the descendants of three of Ham's sons, Mizraim, Phut, and Cush, migrated there."[35] The text goes on to explain that the descendants of Phut inhabited the Sahara, "Mizraim became Egypt," and the descendants of Cush settled west of modern Ethiopia.[36] After factual material about the ancient Sumerians, sixth-graders read:

> What a difference between our God and theirs! Ours is the Creator, not something that has been created. Our God can be reached anywhere at any time, not just from the top of a high building. Our God is the living, loving God of heaven. Who is able to hear and answer the prayers of His children. He is not a frightening part of our imagination or of nature.[37]

On occasion, in keeping with fundamentalist theology, the authors include explicitly millennialist passages. For example, a School of Tomorrow/Accelerated Christian Education booklet tells high school students reading about the modern Middle East that:

> When Jesus Christ came to Earth, He came as Israel's promised Messiah, but Israel refused to accept Him. John 1:11 states, "He came unto his own, and his own received him not." After their rejection of Christ, the Jews were scattered and the nation of Israel ceased to exist. It was not until 1948, after World War II and the Holocaust carried out by Adolf Hitler against the Jews, that Israel was reborn as a

nation. Not realizing that He has already come, Orthodox Jews continue to look for their Messiah. As the end time prophesied in the Bible draws near, many Jews are now turning to Jesus Christ and accepting Him as their Messiah.[38]

At the end of a discussion of the Yom Kippur War, another School of Tomorrow/Accelerated Christian Education booklet tells students that "the eyes of the world continue to be focused on the Near East. There the final events in human history will one day be enacted in accordance with the plan of God."[39] Not surprisingly, the textbooks and materials from all three publishers include numerous citations to and quotations from the Bible. Virtually without exception, Biblical quotations come from the King James version. Sprinkled throughout the texts are lectures to the students about right conduct and correct beliefs. Often these messages are explicitly religious in nature and use second- or third-person pronouns, though first-person pronouns are used occasionally.[40] For example, the author of A Beka's world history text asks senior high school students, "Do you begin to see the consequences of rebelling against God? Do you begin to see the results of humanism, putting man in place of or above God?"[41] One of the School of Tomorrow/Accelerated Christian Education senior high school English booklets comments:

> The problem is that we, you and I, have sinned. We are sinners. That means that we have inherited a disposition toward sin, and we have cooperated with that perverse nature within us. Man, because he is a sinner, does not want to quit sinning. Lollipops, to many, taste better than spinach. But lollipops, sweet as they are, will finally kill us. The same is true about sin. It is enjoyable for a short time, . . . but finally it will do us in. "When it is finished," the Bible says, "[it] bringeth forth death" (James 1:15). So we must recognize that the pursuing of evil — living according to our lower, sinful nature — is of course to be resisted. We must not drop into evil and its consequent ruin.[42] [ellipsis and brackets in the original]

These comments are part of the one-page expository discussion following excerpts from *Macbeth*.

The authors of all books and materials from the three publishers interpose persuasive material with factual material. Thus a seventh-grade Bob Jones world history textbook includes the following statements in its discussion of modern medicine and genetic engineering: "Through genetic engineering (or changing), scientists hope to prevent many abnormalities in unborn children. This may sound good but part of their goal is someday to make a 'perfect' human race. Some scientists believe that if man is physically perfect, he will be totally perfect."[43] The authors of A Beka's seventh-grade world history textbook write that "the 20th century has also brought forward much 'popular' music, particularly rock music, which, with its anti-intellectual emphasis on sensuality, has become a symbol for our times."[44] Moving on to modern art, the author combines this tendency to editorialize with a religious, millennialist assertion.

> Artists in the 20th century have continued to produce a wide variety of beautiful works. However, many modern artists have expressed a disturbing attempt to escape from reason, order, and reality. In their works, they express the rebellion, immorality, pride, and delusion that God said would characterize the last days (2 Tim. 3:1-7).[45]

Discussing the influence of the Enlightenment in France, 10th-graders read that "some of France's most prominent thinkers saw through the hypocrisy of Romanism and rightfully rejected the distorted version of Christianity it represented. Unfortunately, they rejected God altogether and became active atheists, leading the people into the trap of humanism."[46] As these examples illustrate, frequently statements that support conservative religious or political positions appear to be grafted onto unrelated discussions. Negative treatment of certain groups on the basis of their religious or political affiliations takes the form of explicit or thinly veiled disparaging comments, as well as more subtle methods, such as unbalanced or omitted coverage. For example, A Beka's sixth-grade social studies book includes laudatory coverage of Jeanne d'Albret, a hero of the French

Huguenots and the mother of Henry IV, in a highlighted, illustrated text box that covers two-thirds of a page, but the book
devotes only seven lines to Joan of Arc.[47] As I will demonstrate
further in Chapter Two, the texts discuss the suffering of
Protestant martyrs at great length and correctly attribute such suffering to Roman Catholic persecution; however, they omit any
counterbalancing examination of Protestant atrocities against
Catholics. The same pattern holds true for Protestant and
Catholic missionaries. In a few instances Roman Catholic missionary activities are disparaged and in one case mocked.

Although most of the negative coverage of religious groups is
focused on Roman Catholics and non-Western religions,
Protestant churches also are disparaged if they fail to conform to
conservative orthodoxy. The higher criticism of late 19th century
Germany and the churches that adapted it are portrayed as
responsible, at least in part, for the rise of Nazism. "Most of the
German people had by this time [World War I] rejected all but an
empty form of their Christian heritage and had accepted
Modernism almost without question. The vacuum left by this
rejection of *true* Christianity was destined to bring terror and
destruction to Germany" (emphasis added).[48] In discussing the
Colonial Anglican church, the authors of a Bob Jones text speak
of the "spiritual coldness" that resulted from an influx of high
church influences.[49] The teacher's notes explain that "many
Christians have difficulty properly understanding and appreciat-
ing the Anglican church (or Episcopal church, as it is known in
America)" and that "modern Christians would do well not to
approach the Anglican/Episcopal church uncritically but they
should discern what is of value in its history," thus subtly implying that Anglicans and Episcopalians are not Christian.[50]

Another technique used to shape discussions is to let critics
speak virtually unanswered. Much innuendo is inserted by using
comments made by "some people" or "some critics." The arguments of the proponents of a particular point of view are not
included. Thus disfavored religious and political groups are not
allowed to speak for themselves, but the comments or viewpoints

of their critics are included. The following statement illustrates the use of this technique while employing the word *many*: "The belief of many liberals is that everything is relative and constantly changing, leaving man to create his own values."[51] Sometimes the authors use "some people" comments to disparage a mainstream, scholarly, or moderate position. Quoting from Ringenberg, the authors of A Beka's 10th-grade world history text include the following statements: "Apart from the Bible, historians have been unable to trace a creditable history of things to their beginning. . . . While some skeptical historians have loudly denied this testimony, it has commended itself to the faith of millions of people in every generation."[52] Here, the "some skeptical historians" construction allows the authors to cast aspersions on secular historians.

In a number of instances, a group is treated negatively by association. For example, liberalism is explicitly condemned, and then the term *liberal* is applied to other groups. For example, in one of the passages above, the authors contend that the contemporary Anglican/Episcopal community, like other nonevangelical, nonfundamentalist denominations, is tainted by liberalism. "Like most other modern 'mainline' denominations, the Anglican church today is dominated by theological liberalism."[53] In Chapters Two and Three I will examine further the use of *liberal* to disparage individuals, groups, policies, and judicial decisions.

Humanism is another word that is described in negative terms and then applied to groups, movements, and in rare instances individuals. Students already have read that humanism is:

> yet another expression of man's rebellion against God [and] the worship of man. Humanism is the age-old attempt of man to exalt himself in place of or above God. The humanist tries to build up man by ignoring his accountability to God. . . . Since the Tower of Babel, humanism has appeared in many civilizations around the world, and its consequences have always been the same: decline and ultimate ruin.[54]

An example of such decline and ruin is given later in the book when the authors describe the cause of Nazism, which "demonstrat[ed] the spiritual and moral bankruptcy of a nation that accepts the teachings of Darwinism, socialism and humanism."[55] Now when students read that "secular humanism became prevalent in America's public schools and government and the Bible were cast aside" or when they read that the United Nations "continues to pursue the humanistic, utopian goals of its founders," they have been alerted to what is at stake.[56] Students using the School of Tomorrow/Accelerated Christian Education booklets as their textbooks learn a similar definition of humanism and then see it applied to President Franklin Roosevelt and to other liberals and progressives and their policies: "The New Deal programs were based on the humanistic, socialistic philosophy that the 'end justifies the means'."[57] Another charge: Humanists mistakenly supported the League of Nations and criticized fundamentalist ministers for publicly supporting Herbert Hoover, "a very capable president," in 1928.[58] After reading that increased crime in the 1920s was due in part to "the replacing of Godly values with humanistic values in American schools," students are told that "the man who introduced humanism in to the educational system was John Dewey."[59]

The texts elide Darwinism (and evolution generally), religious liberalism, communism and socialism, and political liberalism.[60] For example, in a section titled, "The Beginning of Britain's Decline," 10th-graders read: "By the turn of the 20th century, the faith, energy, and morality of the British people were under attack by the false philosophies of Darwinism, socialism, and modernism."[61] Recall, too, the linkage of Darwinism, socialism, and humanism was cited as a primary, if not *the* primary, cause of the rise of National Socialism. These movements and philosophies are, as we have seen, described as great evils; and it is not unreasonable to assume that students would tend to associate the movements with each other and then infer that the many people, churches, groups, movements, and policies labeled "liberal" or "socialistic" also deserve condemnation on religious, as well as political, grounds.

A Beka and Bob Jones elementary and secondary textbooks and School of Tomorrow/Accelerated Christian Education booklets present a view of the world that differs substantially from that of most Americans, including many conservatives. In the following chapters I will examine in depth what these books teach the children who use them. Chapter Two focuses on how they handle information related to American government and politics. Chapter Three deepens this discussion by examining their presentation of constitutional jurisprudence. In Chapters Four and Five, I turn to how they portray other religious faiths, especially Roman Catholicism (Chapter Four) and non-Western religions (Chapter Five), including Islam, Hinduism, Buddhism, and the indigenous religious traditions of North America, Africa, and Australia.

Notes

1. Sidney E. Mead, *The Lively Experiment: The Shaping of Christianity in America* (New York: Harper & Row, 1963), p. 66; James W. Fraser, *Between Church and State: Religion and Public Education in a Multicultural America* (New York: St. Martin's, Griffin, 1999), p. 20.
2. For a further discussion of the issue of loss and dispossession as an impetus for conservative ideology and activism, see Martin Durham, *The Christian Right, the Far Right, and the Boundaries of American Conservatism* (Manchester, England, and New York: Manchester University Press, 2000), pp. 168-77.
3. James Davison Hunter, *Culture Wars: The Struggle to Define America* (New York: HarperCollins, 1991), pp. 197, 211.
4. Ibid., p. 198.
5. David C. Berliner and Bruce J. Biddle, *The Manufactured Crisis: Myths, Fraud, and the Attacks on America's Public Schools* (Reading, Mass.: Addison-Wesley, 1995).
6. Barbara M. Morris, *Change Agents in the Schools* (Elliot City, Md.: Barbara Morris Report, 1979); Tim LaHaye, *The Battle for the Public Schools: Humanism's Threat to Our Children* (Old Tappan, N.J.: F.H. Revell, 1983); Mel Gabler and Norma Gabler, *What Are They Teaching Our Children?* (Wheaton, Ill.: Victor Books, 1985); Jerry Falwell, *Listen, America!* (Garden City, N.Y.: Doubleday, 1980), p. 190.

7. Pat Robertson, "The New Millennium," in *The Collected Works of Pat Robertson: The New Millennium, The New World Order, The Secret Kingdom* (New York: Inspirational Press, 1994). First published as *The New Millennium: 10 Trends That Will Impact You and Your Family by the Year 2000* (Dallas, Tex.: Word Publishing, 1990).

8. Ibid., pp. 152-55.

9. Berliner and Biddle, op. cit., pp. 299, 310.

10. Marjorie Ledell and Arleen Arnsparger, *How to Deal with Community Criticism of School Change* (Alexandria, Va.: Association for Supervision and Curriculum Development, 1993), p. 16-17.

11. Hunter, op. cit., p. 153.

12. Eugene F. Provenzo Jr., *Religious Fundamentalism and American Education: The Battle for the Public Schools* (Albany: State University of New York Press, 1990).

13. Barbara B. Gaddy, T. William Hall, and Robert J. Marzano, *School Wars: Resolving Our Conflicts over Religion and Values* (San Francisco: Jossey-Bass, 1996).

14. Frances R. A. Paterson, *Legally Related Religious Challenges to Public School Materials, Curricula, and Instructional Activities: The "Impressions" Challenges, 1986-1994* (Ann Arbor, Mich.: University Microfilms, 1997).

15. At the 1998 Christian Coalition "Road to Victory" conference, a panel discussed Christian schools as a separate, parallel system of education. Chip Berlet and Matthew N. Lyons, *Right-Wing Populism in America: Too Close for Comfort* (New York: Guilford, 2000), p. 335.

16. Jerry Falwell, *America Can Be Saved* (Murfreesboro, Tenn.: Sword of the Lord, 1979), p. 52. See also Durham, p. 77.

17. Carper estimated that in 1982 there were between 9,000 and 11,000 Christian day schools in the United States, which is consistent with A Beka's 1998 estimate that 9,000 schools purchased the company's textbooks. James C. Carper and Thomas C. Hunt, eds., *Religious Schooling in America* (Birmingham, Ala.: Religious Education Press, 1984), pp. 114-15; e-mail message from Dennis E. Higgins of A Beka Books, 16 July 1998. Data from the U.S. Department of Education is only marginally more useful. In 1996 Broughman reported that there were 12,222 non-Catholic

sectarian schools serving 1,629,581 students in the United States during 1993-94. *United States Department of Education National Center for Educational Statistics, Private School Universe Survey, 1993-1994* [database online] (Washington, D.C.: U.S. Department of Education, National Center for Educational Statistics, 1996) [cited 30 May 2001], n.p. (Table 1); available from http:// nces.ed.gov/pubs/96143.pdf. In 1995-96 there were 13,081 non-Catholic sectarian schools serving 1,743,791 students. Stephen P. Broughman and Lenore A. Colaciello, *Private School Universe Survey, 1995-1996* [database online] (Washington, D.C.: U.S. Department of Education, National Center for Educational Statistics, 1998) [cited 16 April 1999], p. 5; available from http:// nces.ed.gov/pubs/98229.pdf. In the 1997-98 survey, 13,195 such schools (non-Catholic sectarian schools) served 1,764,447 students. Stephen P. Broughman and Lenore A. Colaciello, *Private School Universe Survey, 1997-1998* [database online] (Washington, D.C.: U.S. Department of Education, National Center for Educational Statistics, 1999) [cited 30 May 2001], p. 5; available from http://nces.ed.gov/pubs99/1999319.pdf. Although some of the schools (e.g., Episcopal, Society of Friends, Jewish, etc.) included in Broughman's category of "other religious" schools would not use the textbooks and curricular materials I examined, many would, including but not limited to, Baptist schools (1,990 in 1993-94; 2,117 in 1995-96; 2,262 in 1997-98), Christian schools without a specified religious orientation (2,416 in 1993-94; 3,359 in 1995-96; 3,371 in 1997-98), and some Missouri Synod Lutheran schools (1,042 in 1993-94; 1,040 in 1995-96; 1,060 in 1997-98), and Assembly of God schools (507 in 1993-94; 513 in 1995-96; 467 in 1997-98). Extrapolating from the survey data, the number of schools in these four groups increased by 20.2%, from 5,955 serving 838,396 students in 1993-94 to 7,160, serving 1,034,152 students in 1997-98. The enrollment of these schools grew by 23%. In contrast, total number of religious schools increased by 2.5%, Roman Catholic schools declined by approximately 2%, and the number of mainline Protestant schools (Episcopal, Evangelical Lutheran Church in America, Methodist, and Presbyterian) increased 5.5%. The percentage change in enrollment figures for these groups is approximately 5% (all religious schools), 1.1% (Roman Catholic schools), and 7.7% (mainline Protestant). U.S. Department of Education, n.p. (Tables 1 and 2); Broughman and Colaciello, *Private School Universe Survey, 1995-1996*, pp. 5-6; Broughman and Colaciello, *Private School Universe Survey, 1997-1998*, pp. 5-6.

18. More than 13,000 children participate in private scholarship programs. Paul E. Peterson, "School Choice: A Report Card," in *Learning from School Choice*, edited by Paul E. Peterson and Bryan Hassel (Washington, D.C.: Brookings Institution, 1998), p. 8.

19. John Gering, "Voucher Battles Head to State Capitals," *Education Week*, 10 July 2002, pp. 1, 24, 25; Tyll Van Geel and William Lowe Boyd, "Vouchers and the Entanglement of Church and State," *Education Week*, 4 September 2002, pp. 46, 49; *Zelman* v. *Simmons-Harris*, 122 S.Ct. 2460 (2002).

20. See Peter W. Cookson Jr., *School Choice: The Struggle for the Soul of American Education* (New Haven, Conn.: Yale University Press, 1994); Bruce Fuller and Richard F. Elmore, eds., *Who Chooses? Who Loses? Culture, Institutions, and the Unequal Effects of School Choice* (New York: Teachers College Press, 1996); Jeffrey R. Henig, *Rethinking School Choice: Limits of the Market Metaphor* (Princeton, N.J.: Princeton University Press, 1994); Frank R. Kemerer, "The Constitutionality of School Vouchers," *West's Education Law Reporter* 101 (August 1995): 17-36; Julie F. Mead, "The Milwaukee Parental Choice Program: An Experiment Challenged," in *25 Years After Yoder: Educational Alternatives*, *Education Law Association Annual Conference* (Seattle, Wash.: Education Law Association, 1997), pp. 31-36; Paul E. Peterson and Bryan C. Hassel, *Learning from School Choice* (Washington, D.C.: Brookings Institution, 1998); John F. Witte, "The Milwaukee Voucher Experiment, " *Educational Evaluation and Policy Review* 20 (Winter 1998): 229-51.

21. See Dan B. Fleming and Thomas C. Hunt, "The World as Seen by Students in Accelerated Christian Education Schools," *Phi Delta Kappan* 68 (March 1987): 518-23; Albert J. Menendez, *Visions of Reality: What Fundamentalist Schools Teach* (Buffalo, N.Y.: Prometheus, 1993).

22. *Jackson* v. *Benson*, 578 NW2d 602 (Wis. 1998), cert. denied, 525 U.S. 997 (1998).

23. Brief for the National Committee for Public Education and Religious Liberty as *Amicus Curiae*, pp. 2, 4-5, 11, 22-28, quoting Ohio Rev. Code Ann. § 3313.976(A)(6) (West 2001). Brief for Council on Religious Freedom et al. as *Amici Curiae*, pp. 28-30, quoting Ohio Rev. Code § 3313.976(A)(6) (West 2001).

24. *Zelman* v. *Simmons-Harris*, 122 S.Ct. 2460, 2503-2508 (2002) (5-4 decision) (Breyer, J., dissenting). It is unclear that the justices found the arguments advanced by the *amici* persuasive because they (and especially Justice Souter) had expressed similar concerns in other Establishment Clause cases decided by the Court.

25. See Alan Peshkin, *God's Choice: The Total World of a Fundamentalist Christian School* (Chicago: University of Chicago Press, 1986); Paul F. Parsons, *Inside America's Christian Schools* (Macon, Ga.: Mercer University Press, 1987); Susan D. Rose, *Keeping Them Out of the Hands of Satan: Evangelical Schooling in America* (New York: Routledge, 1988).

26. Philip G. Altbach et al., eds., *Textbooks in American Society: Politics, Policy, and Pedagogy* (Albany: State University of New York Press, 1991), pp. 8, 237, 243; Michael W. Apple and Linda K. Christian-Smith, *The Politics of the Textbook* (New York: Routledge, 1991), p. 24; Allan C. Ornstein and Francis P. Hunkins, *Curriculum: Foundations, Principles, and Issues*, 3d ed. (Boston: Allyn and Bacon, 1988), pp. 357-59, 391.

27. See Parsons, op. cit., p. 40; Wanda Jean Davis, *The Alternative Educational Systems of Two Fundamentalist Christian School Publishers* (Ann Arbor, Mich.: University Microfilms, 1990). Interested readers may wish to examine these or other textbooks published or distributed by these publishers. Ordering information can be obtained at http://www.abeka.com, http://bjup.com, and http://www.schooloftomorrow.com.

28. Email message from Dennis E. Higgins of A Beka Books, 16 July 1998.

29. Frances R. A. Paterson. "Textbook Use in Schools Participating in Private Scholarship Programs" (1999) (unpublished raw data on file with the author). Note: Some Christian schools, like public schools and other private schools, purchase textbooks from more than one publisher.

30. Robert J. Safransky, "Christian School Textbook Use" (2001) (unpublished raw data on file with the author).

31. Scott James, "Characteristics of Private Schools in Southwest Georgia" (1999) (unpublished raw data on file with author).

32. Higgins, e-mail to author.

33. See Fleming and Hunt, op. cit., p. 518.

34. *Social Studies 1050* (n.p.: Accelerated Christian Education, 1981), p. 26. Berliner also noted an explicit emphasis on the importance of traditional roles for women in School of Tomorrow/Accelerated Christian Education materials. David C. Berliner, "Educational Psychology Meets the Christian Right: Differing Views of Children, Schooling, Teaching, and Learning," *Teachers College Record* 98 (Spring 1997): 399.

35. *Old World History and Geography in Christian Perspective, Teacher Edition* (Pensacola, Fla.: A Beka, 1991), p. 247.

36. *Old World History and Geography*, p. 247. The first chapter of the book divides the human race into the "black race," "red race," "brown race," "yellow race," and "white race," who are "all descendants of one of Noah's sons" (p. 38). The text ascribes the existence of the indigenous peoples of Australia and the Americas to the division of "the land mass in the days of Peleg, a grandson of Sem. The Bible says that in his days was the earth divided (Genesis 10:25)" (p. 38).

37. *Old World History and Geography*, pp. 42-43.

38. *Approaching the Twenty-First Century*, Self-Pac® of Basic Education (#108), rev. 1997 (n.p.: Reform Publications, 1996), p. 51.

39. *Social Studies*, Self-Pac® of Basic Education (#107), rev. 1997 (n.p.: Reform Publications, 1974), p. 9.

40. *Heritage Studies for Christian Schools 6*. (Greenville, S.C.: Bob Jones University Press, 1993), p. 50.

41. Jerry H. Combee, *History of the World in Christian Perspective, Teacher Edition*, 3rd ed. (Pensacola, Fla.: A Beka Books, 1995), p. 6.

42. *English IV-3 (1135)*, rev. 1995 (n.p.: Accelerated Christian Education, 1993), p. 26.

43. *World Studies for Christian Schools, Teacher's Edition* (Greenville, S.C.: Bob Jones University Press, 1993), p. 587.

44. Combee, op. cit., p. 398.

45. Ibid., p. 402.

46. George Thompson and Jerry Combee, *World History and Cultures in Christian Perspective*, 2nd ed. (Pensacola, Fla: A Beka, 1997), p. 513.

47. *Heritage Studies for Christian Schools 6*, pp. 48, 51. The text describes the Huguenots as "true Christians," as opposed to the Roman Catholic majority (p. 51).

48. Combee, op. cit., p. 442. For the most part I have included emphasis as it appears in the original without comment. Occasionally, I include the notation, "emphasis in the original," to alert the reader to the fact that I have not added emphasis. In all cases where I have added emphasis not in the original, I have included this information in the text.

49. Timothy Keesee and Mark Sidwell, *United States History for Christian Schools, Teacher's Edition*, 2nd ed. (Pensacola, Fla.: A Beka, 1991), p. 68. This charge of "spiritual coldness" is occasionally leveled at other mainline and liturgical churches. See Albert J. Menendez, "Heretics, All," in *Visions of Reality: What Fundamentalist Schools Teach* (Buffalo, N.Y.: Prometheus, 1993), pp. 8-31.

50. Keesee and Sidwell, op. cit., p. 68. What is "of value" includes three hymns ("Amazing Grace," "Holy, Holy, Holy," and "Rock of Ages") and the King James version of the Bible. The background material distinguishes between the "many people and movements with the Anglican community [that] have held closely to orthodox Protestantism" and "the church's adherence to certain standard forms of worship and traditional vestments [that] leave the impression that Anglicanism is somehow 'Roman Catholic'" (p. 68).

51. Thompson and Combee, op. cit., p. 445. This statement immediately follows an assertion that conservatives believe in "*absolute standards established by God* — eternal values that need to be conserved" (p. 445).

52. Ibid., p. 7, quoting Loyal R. Ringenberg, *The Living Word in History* (Broadview, Ill.: Gibbs, 1974), pp. 15-17.

53. Ibid., p. 68.

54. Ibid., p. 5.

55. Ibid., p. 500.

56. Ibid., pp. 513, 506. There is actually not too much danger that students would be lulled into a false sense of security regarding the

United Nations, even if the authors had omitted the term *humanistic*, because they go on to state that "at the very heart of the United Nations is a collectivist philosophy that opposes the individual freedoms cherished in free nations like the United States [and whose] founders claim[ed] to seek world peace while laying the groundwork for a totalitarian, one world government" (p. 506).

57. *Social Studies 1094*, rev. 1998 (n.p.: Accelerated Christian Education, 1990), p. 5.
58. *Social Studies 1093*, rev. 1998 (n.p.: Accelerated Christian Education, 1990), p. 28; *Social Studies 1094*, p. 4; *Social Studies 1093*, p. 23.
59. *Social Studies 1093*, p. 23.
60. See section, "Liberals as Godless Secular Humanists," in Berlet and Lyons, op. cit., pp. 239-41.
61. Thompson and Combee, op. cit., p. 378.

CHAPTER TWO

Deluded Democrats, Liberal Villains, and Conservative Heroes

In 1987 Dan Fleming and Thomas Hunt examined School of Tomorrow/Accelerated Christian Education (ACE) materials used in approximately 5,000 evangelical and fundamentalist Christian schools and concluded that the materials they examined were biased and "appear[ed] to distort truth to fit a particular political/religious belief."[1] Fleming and Hunt examined six social studies booklets (referred to as "units") from School of Tomorrow/Accelerated Christian Education. More recently I examined social studies textbooks published by A Beka Press for grades 4 through 12 and by Bob Jones University Press for grades 3 through 12, and 84 social studies booklets published or distributed by School of Tomorrow/Accelerated Christian Education. The discussion in this chapter is primarily drawn from these publishers' civics and American history textbooks and related materials. Like Fleming and Hunt a decade earlier, I found the texts were biased toward a particular point of view that was overwhelmingly conservative. Shorn of the text that makes them uniquely textbooks — long passages about the influence of Prince Metternich, pictures of medieval cathedrals, descriptions of the geography of Thailand, and explanations of the history and workings of the electoral college — these books become indistinguishable from the literature of the Religious Right. Delete from this mass the statements based on religious faith and what remains is a series of ideological statements that could easily pass for partisan campaign literature, albeit without reference to a particular election or endorsement of a particular candidate.

General Treatment of Government and Politics

As I discussed in Chapter One, Christian school textbooks differ from the secular materials used in public and other nonpublic and religious schools in several ways. In terms of their approach to political issues, several characteristics are particularly salient. First, they frequently use descriptors for people, groups, and movements that make clear to the reader that some are more acceptable than others and that many are simply unacceptable. Many short sections use the term *liberal* in their titles and then criticize the actions or policies discussed. For example, in a subsection titled "A Liberal Supreme Court," eighth-graders read that "the Supreme Court made several liberal decisions in the 1970s, indicating the moral decline of the nation as a whole."[2] High school students learn that "another trend that has resulted from the new emphasis on rights among liberal-leaning groups is the tendency to legitimate perversion."[3] In A Beka's world history textbooks the term *liberal* is tied to German higher criticism and to the belief in evolution. Both are thoroughly castigated. Seventh-graders read:

> By the late 19th century, the seeds of Modernism, or religious liberalism, had taken root in Germany, the Land of the Reformation. Theologians in German universities denied the authority of the Bible, exulting their own reason above God's word and teaching that the Bible was just a collection of myths and legends with few historical facts. They *denied the basic doctrines of Christianity,* including Christ's deity, man's sin nature, and the reality of heaven and hell.[4]

Bob Jones textbooks and School of Tomorrow/Accelerated Christian Education materials contain similar but more nuanced statements on the subject. In A Beka's eighth-grade U.S. history book, a text box titled "Political Parties" is more overtly political and defines a liberal as:

a person who believes government should have more control over people's lives, that government through taxes should provide more of people's needs, and that Biblical traditional values are not strong considerations. [By contrast] a conservative is a person who believes that the government's main responsibility is to protect people and property from crime and from foreign invaders, give people freedom to handle their own economic responsibilities, and conserve the traditional, Biblical standards of right and wrong upon which America was built.[5]

The authors acknowledge that liberals and conservatives exist in both parties but point out that liberals are more likely to be found in the Democratic Party and conservatives in the Republican Party. Still, the implication is clear. Right-thinking people, people with "good" values would be conservatives and by extension are more likely to be Republicans. The publishers 10th-grade world history text defines a conservative as "a person who wants to conserve a standard [that] is desirable if the standard is good (the Bible, the U.S. Constitution, Judeo-Christian ethics) and undesirable if the standard is bad (Marxism, false religions, immorality)."[6] *"American and other Western conservatives believe there are eternal values that need to be preserved in human thought and action; they also seek to preserve the Judeo-Christian heritage that has made the West great"* (emphasis in the original).[7] Conservative principles include the belief that *"there are absolutes established by God"* and that "people will be happier if they maintain private responsibility for their own property, families and futures [but] if government controls these things the result will be poverty and tyranny" (emphasis in the original).[8] By contrast, liberalism "begin[s] with the unBiblical idea that man is basically good" and leads to "slavery, first to man's unbridled passions (anarchy) and eventually to an all-powerful totalitarian state."[9] "Modern liberalism has had many tragic consequences — war, tyranny, and despair — for mankind."[10] The conclusion is inescapable. Liberalism and liberals are misguided at best and thoroughly evil at worst, and liberalism is contrary to God's will.

A School of Tomorrow/Accelerated Christian Education American government booklet issues an unmistakable call for students to support and vote for conservative candidates. Students read in a highlighted text box that "as Bible Believers, we cannot isolate ourselves from our government. We must become involved in the political processes by voting for candidates who support our conservative, Biblical principles. . . ."[11]

Second, Christian school textbooks include and exclude individuals and groups — that is, conservatives are cited and quoted with approval, while liberals are given less coverage, omitted, or treated in a critical fashion. In Chapter One, I illustrated how this technique was used with historical figures, such as Jeanne d'Albret and Joan of Arc. Later, in Chapter Four, I will examine how it is used *vis-à-vis* historical and contemporary figures based on their religion: Roman Catholic or Protestant. Here, the "fault line" for disparate coverage is based on political ideology. In A Beka's fourth-grade history text, Supreme Court Justice Clarence Thomas is discussed in laudatory terms: "Through his own hard work and God-given ability, he earned a law degree and achieved several important government positions."[12] Justice Thurgood Marshall, on the other hand, is not mentioned at all in the publisher's fourth-grade book. The text includes 22 lines (including an eight-line quotation) about Clarence Thomas and a color photograph of him.[13] Bob Jones' civics book includes a quotation from Justice Marshall (labeled as a "liberal activist") that the text describes as "an example of . . . a narrow, arrogant judgment."[14] This disparity of coverage extends to illustrations. As noted (see endnote 13) Clarence Thomas is pictured in A Beka's fourth-, eighth-, and 11th-grade textbooks, while Thurgood Marshall is pictured only in the 11th-grade text. The eighth-grade text contains a chapter covering the years 1980 through 1994. In this chapter the following individuals are pictured: Ronald Reagan (three times), Margaret Thatcher, Thomas Sowell, Oliver North, Sandra Day O'Connor, George Bush (twice), Dan Quayle (with Bush), Colin Powell (with his wife), Norman Schwarzkopf, Clarence Thomas, Bill Clinton, Hillary Clinton (with President

Clinton).[15] Thus, Republicans or conservatives constitute 13 of the 16 individually identified individuals (excluding Mrs. Powell, who is not identified by name) shown in color photographs.

Third, in Christian school textbooks, material that conveys the opinions of the authors is presented in discrete sections, in separate paragraphs, and in sentences within paragraphs of factual information. For example, in a subsection discussing the Depression and the presidency of Herbert Hoover, the following two sentences appear: "By 1932, one in every four workers — 13 million people — was unemployed. Alarmed by socialist propaganda from the media and certain liberal politicians, many Americans *blamed President Hoover for the Depression and looked for a change in leadership*."[16] In short, the election of Franklin Roosevelt did not represent a genuine desire for change in leadership but resulted from a manipulation of the electorate by the media and "liberal politicians."

Fourth, in discussing both social and economic issues, Christian school textbooks emphasize individual responsibility and weakness over structural causes of human suffering and inequality. For example, a civics book tells high school students that "modern liberalism tends to have an un-Biblical view of man's nature, believing that man is basically good and that evil is the result of environment not inherent depravity. Therefore, by extension liberal positions today, particularly on social issues, are generally further from the Scripture than conservative positions."[17] The only structural changes necessary to ameliorate social and economic problems are for individuals and society in general to adapt Biblically based values.

In some cases, the placement of subjects allows them to be de-emphasized. For example, Bob Jones's eighth-grade American history text briefly mentions lynching in two widely separated sections. Neither is included in the material related to Reconstruction or the post-Civil War period. In one instance, the text notes that Ray Stannard Baker (one of several muckrakers who, though they exposed "hidden problems," had "political and religious views [that] were not sound") "attacked lynching, executing blacks without trial."[18] Sixty-five pages later, the text mentions lynching again — in connection with Franklin Roosevelt: "Although Roosevelt refused to support civil rights regulations and an anti-lynching law in 1936, he still got black support."[19] It is not possible to determine whether this type of structuring is intentional; however, the absence of any discussion of white complicity in the lynching of African Americans, coupled with the use of the subject to denigrate FDR, cannot have been an oversight. A similar unusual subject matter arrangement allows the author of A Beka's fourth-grade U.S. history text to separate discussions of civil rights and the advancement of minorities from any discussion of the presidents under which they occurred. Intentional or not, this placement has the effect of denying both Republican and Democratic presidents credit for progress on these issues. Still, the author does find praise for Republican presidents, but few good words to say about Democratic ones, especially since Democratic support of minority rights goes unmentioned.

Fifth, in Christian school textbooks theocracy is portrayed as the ideal form of government. The A Beka civics textbook begins by asserting that the most perfect form of government is a theocracy: "All governments are ordained of God, but none compare to government by God, theocracy."[20] "Under a theocracy, perfect justice and equity flourish because God is perfectly just and righteous."[21] Even though ancient Israel did not embody elements of democracy, the authors hold up a government in which "the priesthood and special rulers . . . mediated" God's rules as an ideal state.[22] What is troubling about this line of thought is that students may come to believe that a state in which individuals interpret God's laws would be one that approaches, however imperfectly, this ideal of theocracy. Both the A Beka and Bob Jones civics texts emphasize that humanity's sinfulness dictates the need for restraints imposed by government: "God delegates authority to governments to accomplish their 'primary purpose' [that of] restraint — restraining man's sinful activity."[23] A similar sentiment is expressed in A Beka's civics book: "Ever since the fall, man has needed outward limits and restraints on the expression of his sinful nature. God's original purpose for government was to punish the evil and reward the good."[24] The text goes on to define the "perfect government" as a theocracy, which existed in ancient Israel and imperfectly in Puritan New England. Both texts praise the government of Puritan New England as particularly godly and lament its spiritual and concomitant temporal decline. In the opinion of the authors of the A Beka text, Puritan New England "floundered because . . . man's sinful nature makes theocracy impossible in the present world."[25]

Sixth, the Christian school texts emphasize the evils of communism, both in the language they use to describe the communist system generally and its pernicious effects, past and present, and in the amount of coverage they give to these topics. Socialism also is strongly condemned. Fourth-graders read that "in some countries there is no such choice [referring to an example about the availability of toys at a toy store given on the previous page]. The government owns the factories and stores, sets prices, decides who will be allowed to work, and selects who gets the profits. Such countries are called socialistic."[26] Fourth-grade teachers are instructed to "Point out that a socialist government . . . represents a master/slave relationship with the government making all the decisions and controlling all the businesses."[27] The authors tend to shortcut discussions of the distinctions between socialism and communism. For example, A Beka's senior high school civics book states that "history shows socialism gradually opens the door to Communism" and that "socialism is but a halfway house to Communism; what Communists seek by peaceful means — legislation, regulation, and taxation."[28] Four pages later a text box enumerates the dangers of communism, and by the authors' reasoning, socialism:

> Darwinism and Communism both support the idea that man is autonomous (responsible to no one but himself) and must attempt build a "brave new world" without reference to God or God's law. . . . Communists are drifting in a sea of relativism, a consequence of atheism. No God means no law,

no law means no absolute standards of good and evil or right or wrong. . . . Communism denies that man is God's creature and image bearer, that man has a soul.[29]

The nuclear family stands in the way of communist domination; therefore, "It is no wonder that Satan hates the family and has hurled his venom against it in the form Communist ideology."[30] Bob Jones's civics text does distinguish between different types of socialism, for example, "European social democracy," "worker-managed socialism," and communism ("the most radical form of socialism") as forms of a "command economy."[31] On the page following this information is a section devoted to Karl Marx, titled "Karl Marx: The Socialist Solution."[32] And while the author states explicitly that "there is nothing inherently Christian about capitalism, and there is nothing inherently godless about socialism," he devotes several paragraphs to explicating why, based on the parable of the talents found in the book of Matthew, capitalism clearly reflects the values of the New Testament.[33] A School of Tomorrow/Accelerated Christian Education booklet covering Colonial America acknowledges that the Pilgrims practiced a form of socialism through communal ownership of land but uses its discussion to reinforce a religiously grounded view of socialism as immoral:

> The failures of these colonial communal ventures should be object lesson to today's advocates of planned socialist economies. God never sanctioned Communism. The early church practiced a limited form of socialism, but it was (1) voluntary, (2) short-lived, and (3) for a specific situation. It was never taught as a doctrine of Christianity. Socialism promotes laziness which is definitely contrary to the Scripture.[34]

Another booklet attributes socialism (one of several "radical systems of thought") to "the bad conditions of the early Industrial Revolution."[35] Karl Marx espoused a "different kind of socialism . . . called scientific socialism."[36] Socialism split into two divisions: "moderate or 'right-wing' socialism and communist or

'left-wing' socialism."[37] The former "sought to establish socialism by peaceful, democratic means while the communist social-
ists advocated violent revolution to overthrow established
governments and substitute communist governments."[38]

In light of the linking of socialism and communism, the use of
the terms *socialism* and *socialistic* in connection with Democratic presidents and their policies is particularly problematic.
For example, in A Beka's senior high school world history book,
the authors state that:

> A serious flaw developed in American culture during the
> Cold War period as America began to drift away from the
> institutions and heritage that made her great. For example,
> the U.S. government continued to move toward socialism
> following the "New Deal"; under the Kennedy, Johnson, and
> Carter Administrations, government spending grew enor-
> mously as welfare programs sapped the economy and re-
> sulted in a heavier tax burden upon the American people.[39]

Often these texts present their consistently conservative worldview by labeling Democratic presidents and their policies as
"socialistic." In fact, this is such a pervasive strategy that it merits
a closer look in the next section.

Political Figures and Their Treatment

The treatment of elected officials and political figures depends
on their ideology. Frequently, they are identified as "liberal" (and
in some cases "socialist" or "socialistic") or "conservative."
Senator Joseph McCarthy is treated in neutral, even mildly positive, fashion. For example: "What was often ignored in the out-
rage over McCarthy's methods was the reality of the Communist
threat in America."[40] Similarly, the John Birch Society is treated
with mild approval because the organization "held that Communist subversion affected high public officials in the country and it
questioned the patriotism of those who pursued the policy of
peaceful coexistence with the Soviet Union."[41] This pattern holds
true for more contemporary figures as well. For example, the

achievements and views of Phyllis Schlafly are described in a highlighted text box. Schlafly, "a wise woman" who took "abuse" was "virtually hissed" at by "female reporters," "shrieked" at by "a radical feminist," and "assaulted [and] sometimes spat upon . . . kept her calm, even, and always courteous tones" and "stated her arguments in crisp tones supported by a wealth of research."[42]

The pattern of treatment also applies to Republican and Democratic politicians. By and large, Republicans are given favorable and sometimes laudatory coverage. The more conservative they are, the more approvingly the texts portray them. Democrats are given negative treatment. Ronald Reagan and his policies are described in warm, glowing terms: "Prime Minister Thatcher and President Reagan shared the same vision of strong traditional values, limited government and strength toward communism. Conservatives had long argued for a return to traditional values and common sense government."[43] Reagan's policies are praised: "Critics labeled these policies, 'Reaganomics,' not realizing that Reagan's ideals were part of the traditional principles that had made America great."[44] During the Reagan Administration, "sound conservative thinking flourished. . . ."[45] A School of Tomorrow/Accelerated Christian Education booklet explicitly links religion to the outcome of the 1988 election: "President Reagan's policies were often based on Constitution and on Scriptural [sic] principles and nearly 54 percent of the voters chose to continue those policies."[46] Likewise, A Beka's 11th-grade American history book connects Reagan's right religious beliefs to his election as president: "He expressed a sincere desire to return America to the traditional values (Biblical values such as moral purity, honesty, respect for human life) that had made America great."[47]

It is difficult to overstate the amount of approval and praise, which occasionally borders on the effusive, for Reagan that is expressed by the authors of all three publishers' materials. George H.W. Bush and Bob Dole are approached in a somewhat cooler manner. The activities and personal qualities of Trent Lott, Newt Gingrich, and other conservative Republicans, such as Phil

Gramm, Bill Bennett, Pat Robertson, and Dick Armey, also are treated in positive fashion, while students read that Bill Clinton was "a double dealing liberal president," whose conduct in the Whitewater and Lewinsky matters is described disapprovingly for elementary, junior high, and high school students.[48] For example, A Beka's fourth-grade U.S. history book omits any reference to the Lewinsky scandal, but alludes to "possible abuses of security at the White House and use of illegal campaign funds."[49] In the publisher's eighth-grade American history book, this statement becomes "rumors circulated of scandalous behavior, including an adulterous affair and illegal business dealings."[50] Gossip or news reports concerning similar conduct on the part of conservative Republican officeholders is absent. In a section titled "A Liberal Agenda," Mrs. Clinton is described as being engaged in a "crusade" for "socialized medicine," although "conservatives warned" that the "national health care plan (socialized medicine)" would result in "substandard health care."[51] Following this discussion the authors include a short section on Tax Freedom Day, the implication being that high taxation can be laid solely, or at least primarily, at the feet of the Democratic president and liberals generally.

Nor is the explicit criticism of Democratic presidents limited to President Clinton. In general, more recent Democratic presidents are criticized most strongly, although Roosevelt is treated more harshly than Truman or Carter. FDR's "New Deal programs were based on humanistic, socialistic philosophy that the 'end justifies the means'."[52] "Although President Roosevelt did provide jobs for many Americans, in the process he did more than any other President to move America toward socialism."[53] Bob Jones' senior high school American history book opines that "the wide popularity evoked by [President Roosevelt's] socialistic schemes certainly posed a threat to America's economic foundations."[54] Truman's Fair Deal, with its "incipient socialism and welfarism," resulted in Republican victories in the 1950 off-year election.[55] The text ignores the fact that the party that does not occupy the White House typically gains in off-year elections. A School of

Tomorrow/Accelerated Christian Education booklet echoes this view of Truman: "As Congress became more conservative, President Truman became more liberal. He supported labor unions and such socialistic programs as government aid to farmers, expanding social security, and providing federal housing aid."[56] Kennedy is remembered for the "mysteries surrounding his death."[57] Of his assassination, the authors write, "John F. Kennedy's sudden death at the hands of an assassin made him *seem to be* a martyr" (emphasis added).[58] One of Kennedy's signature programs, the Peace Corps, resulted in "some . . . volunteers . . . introduc[ing] state-sponsored birth control, distrust of Christian missionaries, disregard for private property, and dependence on government socialism."[59] Johnson's Great Society was "well-intentioned" but led to "higher taxes [that] drained money from individuals and businesses to fund programs that destroyed the work ethic among the poor while eroding the self-sufficiency of the American family."[60] Jimmy Carter's presidency is discussed in a section titled "The Ineffectual Presidency," which contrasts to a text box extolling "The Reagan Magic."[61] Bob Jones' civics textbook notes that "newly created judgeships as well as the usual vacancies allowed Carter to fill hundreds of openings nationwide with liberal Democrats."[62] A School of Tomorrow/Accelerated Christian Education booklet describes the Carter presidency:

> The Carter Administration gave away the Panama Canal, downgraded our relationship with Taiwan, pardoned the American draft dodgers, and established the Department of Energy and the Education Department. All of those actions subsequently proved to be very unpopular with the American electorate. In addition, the United States experienced further serious energy and economic "crunches" and America's military strength declined alarmingly. It is also sad to note that under President Carter, a man who publicly proclaimed himself to be a born again Christian, government attacks on Christian schools, Christian children's homes, Christian day care centers, and churches rose astonishingly.[63]

Like FDR and Truman, President Clinton is linked to socialism. "As socialism seemed to be weakening in Eastern Europe and the Soviet Union, it strengthened its grasp on the American people when Democrat Bill Clinton won the election of 1992."[64]

The Treatment of Social Issues

Both the civics and history textbooks repeatedly state that America is in a moral decline and blame a variety of secular and religious causes for this condition. Flippantly, one might be tempted to say that "all the usual suspects" are presented: secular humanism, man's sinful nature, public education, big government encouraging a diminution of personal responsibility, and so on. For example, Bob Jones' civics text states that "secular humanistic thought, which puts man at the center of all things, now provides a basis for public morals, judicial decisions, and social values."[65] Criticism of contemporary culture focuses on alleged breakdowns in social order and family values during the 1960s and 1970s. Eighth-graders read that "although the United States has been a sinless nation, conditions of the 1960s and 1970s saw much open defiance of God's standards" with the result that "hard rock music, drugs, and open immorality continue to plague America."[66] A Beka's high school world history book describes the Cold War era as a time when "America's traditional morality was . . . attacked through literature, cinema, and rock and roll music, with its message of rebellion against all traditional values, restraints, and authority. American young people began to blatantly exhibit a rebellious attitude toward authority."[67] Even after the "hippie" decade of the 1960s, "America's immorality grew worse as abortion and immoral life styles were considered 'normal' by many people."[68] Even fourth-graders receive the same message, albeit in more subtle terms, when the section of their American history book devoted to Ronald Reagan is titled "A Return to Patriotism and Family Values."[69]

The importance of the family is underscored again and again; however, the family must conform to God's mandate, which is linked, in turn, to the proper relationship of human beings to government. Governmental authority flows from God to human institutions and to the individuals responsible for ruling others within those institutions [according to] a definite order of command from God to human leaders to their followers. For example, the husband is the head of the wife and the parents are God's representatives to rule their children. Individuals obey God when they submit to and obey the God-appointed authorities over them.[70]

Bob Jones' civics textbook stresses that "Scripture draws clear lines of authority within the home. 'God's ideal' for the home is that the husband exercise his authority and responsibility as a leader [and] the wife is to submit to his authority."[71] Both are to "exercise authority" over their children, who must "willingly submit."[72] Eighth-graders learning American history also learn that "One of Satan's strongest attacks on America and on the church comes from his attacks on the family unit."[73] A School of Tomorrow/Accelerated Christian Education booklet describes the weakening of the family as originating in the Industrial Revolution (producing a "type of fatherlessness") which was then exacerbated by the war work performed by women during the Second World War and by postwar social changes: "As women assumed more responsibilities, men gradually surrendered their Biblical position as head of the home. During the second half of the twentieth century, the dissolution of the American family became statistically evident in increasing divorce rates, illegitimate births, abortions, single parents, and domestic violence."[74] One solution is for private religious organizations to encourage "husbands and fathers [to] provide strong leadership."[75] "The Promise Keepers are evidence of the fact that God and the Bible can still change lives and provide the spiritual leaders our nation needs — without a government program."[76]

Abortion and homosexuality are strongly condemned. The coverage of abortion begins in elementary school materials and increases in both detail and vehemence through the grades. In A Beka's fourth-grade history text, abortion is defined as the "killing of unborn babies"[77] Eighth-graders using Bob Jones textbooks read that the legalization of abortion "indicated a breakdown of national morality" that reflected "a defiance of God's will."[78] Language such as "innocent babies," "grisly procedure," "[l]egalized murder," and "slaughter of unborn babies" is common. Eleventh-graders studying American history are told that, "according to many conservatives, President Clinton's most reprehensible act was his repeated veto of the Partial Birth Abortion Act."[79] After presenting some factual material, the text flatly states, "Clinton's assertion that this type of abortion is necessary to protect the health of the mother is simply not true."[80] In many instances, pro-life arguments are linked to criticism of the Supreme Court's decision in *Roe* v. *Wade*. For example, fourth-graders read that *Roe* v. *Wade* was one of "many liberal court decisions" that occurred during the 1960s and 1970s.[81] Bob Jones' eighth-grade American history textbook opines that, as a result of *Roe* ("a liberal decision on abortion"), "legalized murder destroys nearly a third of all American babies every year."[82] A Beka's civics textbook opines that the Court's decision in *Roe* was an obvious error ("the error of such thinking was obvious") because "the right of any mother to have power of life and death over a child once conceived is much more than a 'right to privacy'; it is the usurpation of God's role in the lives of others, a right that does not reside in the four corners of the Constitution."[83] Bob Jones' civics text includes a highlighted text box describing various abortion procedures in considerable detail.[84] An ACE high school U.S. history booklet informs students that:

> During the sixteen years following that 1973 decision, more than 20 million lives were ended by abortion. That number is more than ten times the number of Americans who have died in all the wars the nation has fought! That number is more than three times the number of Jews that Adolf Hitler exterminated in concentration camps during the Holocaust! The United States of America, founded on the Word of God, had legalized the murder of millions of babies.[85]

Abortion is not only specifically condemned but also explicitly linked to other "sinful" conduct, including homosexuality, which, in turn, is linked to criminal conduct. Because homosexuals engage in "vile affections," their claim to legal protection is unwarranted: "These people have no more claim to special rights than child molesters or rapists," says Bob Jones' senior high school current events textbook.[86] This publisher's civics book also links homosexuality with abortion rights as undeserving of legal protection:

> The tendency to twist evil in order to make it seem good by giving it an acceptable name is nothing new. God warned in Isaiah 5:20, "Woe unto them that call evil good, and good evil." Today when homosexuals call their sin a "sexual preference" that deserves constitutional protection, or abortionists call the destroying of unborn life a freedom of "choice," they are simply calling evil good.[87]

As with abortion, middle and junior high school students are exposed to explicit condemnation of gay people and the "gay lifestyle." Eighth-graders learn that:

> Along with such good causes [the elderly "who may easily be abused by others"] appear despicable movements such as that for "gay rights" for homosexuals. These immoral Americans not only try to excuse their sin as simply another choice of lifestyle but also try to demand special recognition and privilege. Such a situation serves to illustrate man's sinful condition and his great need for the Savior.[88]

By contrast, issues related to race and the civil rights movement are discussed in a more straightforward and objective fashion, though the tone is generally somewhat cool. Very rarely do the authors editorialize. When they do so, the inferences that can be drawn from their statements can be startling. A Beka's 10th-grade American history text subtly implies that Martin Luther King was partially responsible for his own assassination. "On a visit to Memphis, Tennessee, in 1968, [King] was assassinated by James Earl Ray, a gunman who used the violent atmosphere to justify his own racism."[89] The authors of the high school American history book from Bob Jones University place more emphasis on the enslavement of African Americans as a problem, "an ugly situation," and a cause of civil unrest and radicalism than on the nature of the institution itself.[90] The authors de-emphasize the inhumanity of the institution by opining that slavery was not particularly cruel: "A few slave holders were undeniably cruel. Examples of slaves beaten to death were not common, neither were they unknown. The majority of slave holders treated their slaves well."[91] The authors also include a somewhat contrived example of providentialism:

> To help them endure the difficulties of slavery, God gave Christian slaves the ability to combine the African heritage of song with the dignity and power of Christian praise. Through the Negro spiritual, the slaves developed the patience to wait on the Lord and discovered that the truest freedom is freedom from the bondage of sin. By first giving them spiritual freedom, God prepared the slaves for their coming physical freedom.[92]

This passage is consistent with the previously discussed view that individuals are, for the most part, powerless to affect their temporal situations and that structural reforms are relatively unimportant. African Americans were wrong to "push" for desegregation in the courts. They and their liberal supporters "were not willing to wait for a political solution."[93] Bob Jones' high school history textbook also takes this ambiguous approach to its discussion of the Klu Klux Klan. On the one hand, the authors castigate the organization as "feeding on racism and bigotry."[94] On the other hand, the sentence that follows it opines that "the Klan in some areas of the country tried to be a means of reform, fighting the decline in morality and using the symbol of the cross [to] target bootleggers, wife beaters and immoral movies."[95] Eighth-graders reading the publisher's middle school textbook read that "killing blacks who tried to exercise their civil rights" was "more unsavory" than the Klan's "least offensive tactic" of boycotting businesses.[96] By contrast, a School of Tomorrow/Accelerated

Christian Education U.S. history booklet takes an unequivocal anti-Klan stance: "Thousands of innocent victims throughout the South were murdered, beaten and driven from their land by these vigilante groups."[97]

Little attention is paid to the moral ambiguities of the death penalty. A Beka's civics text devotes a few scant lines to the subject. In the opinion of its author, the death penalty was the "first foundational civil ordinance" through which "God ordained civil governments."[98] Those who doubt the death penalty's continuing validity are reminded that the New Testament obligates rulers to "'execute wrath upon him that doeth evil (Rom. 13:4)'."[99] A text box containing a lengthy excerpt from a book published by the Sword of the Lord states that "'the man who pulls the switch when the criminal dies is the agent of God who commanded the death of a murderer'."[100]

The texts are uncompromisingly critical of public education. A School of Tomorrow/Accelerated Christian Education booklet links public education to the nation's religious decline: "There are several reasons why North America has not experienced a great spiritual awakening. The humanist educational system, media, and mindset have trained North Americans to rationalize away much of the Bible and its teaching."[101] Another booklet includes a section titled "Responding to Moral Decay." The first subsection, titled "Biblical education," begins, "After prayer and Bible reading were removed from the public schools in 1962 and 1963, private schools using Biblically based curriculum multiplied rapidly. While government entities seek solutions for the crisis in education, schools dedicated to Biblical education have been providing solutions for nearly three decades."[102] This ignores that many private schools, especially in the South, were formed in the 1960s and 1970s because of the desegregation of the public schools. Many conservatives who are hostile to public education use the term "government schools."[103] A third booklet introduces this terminology: "In a short time, public schools became 'government schools' because governments — local, state, and federal — completely funded and controlled them."[104] A Beka's high school U.S. history textbook presents public education as suffering from a process of deterioration:

> Because basic phonics, traditional math, drill, and repetition had been virtually eliminated from many school curriculums, students were not learning. Grades fell, and a reliable study classified 30% of all public school students as "learning disabled." As the federal government began to hand out large amounts of money to educate these "learning disabled" students, critics suggested that some educators labeled students "learning disabled" in order to qualify for more government aid.[105]

A School of Tomorrow/Accelerated Christian Education booklet on American government shows a one-room schoolhouse bound by chains. Over the door is a sign that reads, "Big Brother Public School." The caption announces that this is "another fine, professionally engineered, state-of-the-art security, high tech, nonreligious, tax-payer funded, federal government school for your [the word, *your*, is crossed out with a red X] our children!"[106]

The Treatment of Economic Issues

In quasi-economic discussions related to poverty and its amelioration, a fatalistic providentialism predominates. The suffering of the poor during the Industrial Revolution is de-emphasized, and in some instances the authors allege that the social reformers of the period exaggerated the squalid conditions of urban industrial workers. The authors present poverty as rooted in personal weakness and ignore or downplay possible structural causes.[107] Organized efforts — including the efforts of the social gospel movement in the late 1800s and early 1900s, of labor unions, and of government programs — are characterized as contrary to God's plan for humanity, injurious to good government, or both. "Many of the solutions offered [by the Progressives] to bonafide problems tended to the erosion of our free and republican political system by further democratizing or socializing it."[108] High school American history booklets produced by School of Tomorrow/Accelerated Christian Education take a somewhat more strident tone: "The Founding Fathers' plan for government, the *Constitution*, included the protection of citizens, the promotion of general welfare, and the provision for a common defense. It did not include the giving of handouts to citizens."[109] In the same section, students read that "like many other government programs, [Medicare and Medicaid] are socialistic [and] Social Security is not a good investment program."[110] The author lists four criticisms of the program:

- Social Security does not provide a rate of return equal to that of private investments.
- Contributions are coerced.
- Individuals may not receive benefits equal to their contributions, while others may receive more than they contributed.
- The program is likely to fail because of administrative costs and the changing ratio of beneficiaries to workers.[111]

The section concludes by implying that Social Security and other government programs to ameliorate poverty are contrary to the Bible: "Scripture plainly teaches that widows, the needy, and others who cannot provide for themselves are to have their needs met [but] God's plan is for these needs to be met first by family members and then by local churches, but not by government."[112]

Unemployment also is caused by personal weakness or the actions of government. Bob Jones' civics text discusses frictional unemployment ("people who become dissatisfied with one job and leave it to seek another, as well as people who have been laid off or fired"), seasonal unemployment, structural unemployment ("they [may] soon become dependent on relatives, charities, or welfare programs and be a permanent drain on society and the economy"), and cyclical unemployment ("government interference brings with it the accompanying controls and problems of a command economy").[113] The author goes on to note the positive effects of a fear of unemployment as "a good incentive for workers to be diligent in their labors. When there is the possibility of being fired or laid off, a worker is less likely to shirk his responsibilities and more apt to be efficient in his services to the business."[114] The market, unencumbered by the restrictions of the minimum wage, is the best solution for employment problems. A Beka's eighth-grade U.S. history text echoes this negative assessment of human nature, which can be linked to the underlying theological premise of humanity's innate depravity. Speaking of welfare programs enacted during President Kennedy's administration, the authors write that "because it is human nature to try to get something for nothing, many people took advantage of government handouts."[115]

Repeatedly, the textbooks extol the virtues of free markets and free trade and argue against anything more than a minimal role for government in economic matters, consumer protection, and environmental regulation. Government, like moderate or liberal politicians, is often criticized and almost never portrayed in a favorable light. Even in the rare instances in which government is depicted as having benevolent motives, it is portrayed as misguided and its actions are described as having significant detrimental effects. One singular exception to this generalization is the discussion of Prohibition. The textbooks argue that Prohibition was a proper action for the federal government to take and that its failure was a consequence of human frailty and sinfulness. When discussing economic matters, the texts devote a great deal of space to pointing out the weaknesses of communism (often elided with socialism) and mixed economies, generally by contrasting these systems with capitalism.

The texts, especially those from A Beka, view taxation, especially the progressive income tax, as a necessary evil. High school students read that "good jobs were produced during the Reagan administration" because "business owners [paid] fewer taxes [and so] they had more money to build new offices and factories."[116] The authors opine that "when people . . . are able to keep most of their money rather having it taxed away, they have the freedom to spend or invest [and become] more self-sufficient, fill[ed] with a sense of responsibility, [and] reward[ed for] their efforts to better themselves."[117] Embedded in a discussion of the Clinton presidency is a subsection titled "More Taxes," in which the authors of A Beka's eighth-grade American history book dis-

cuss Tax Freedom Day and blame high taxes on welfare programs: "Much of the taxes paid by hard-working Americans
funded government welfare programs, because many Americans
had become dependent on government handouts which gradually
take away self-respect, initiative, and personal freedoms."[118] In
Bob Jones' civics textbook, the teacher's chapter review questions related to economics point out that "leaders in the command
economy complain about unfair income distribution . . . heavily
tax the rich [and as a result] people lose incentive to work hard
[and] laziness is rewarded."[119] Later, the author cites the parable
of the talents, found in Matthew, for the proposition that the progressive income tax is antithetical to Jesus' teachings in the New
Testament: "Although our Lord was teaching a spiritual truth
about the believer's stewardship . . . ," the parable can be applied
to economics. "Each servant was given different amounts of
money; no attempt was made to redistribute the wealth and equal-
ize the servants' holdings."[120] The publisher's U.S. history books
do not present such strong opinions about the federal income tax.
More subtle statements convey the authors' disapproval.
Discussing the passage of the 16th Amendment, the income tax is
portrayed as taking money from the very rich "and us[ing] it, *the-
oretically*, for the benefit all Americans" (emphasis added).[121] The
authors instruct teachers to point out "on behalf of progressives
. . . that at the time they were not likely to see the dangers of big
government [but] since the New Deal of the 1930s, [we have]
been able to see some of the dangers of the progressive reliance
on government."[122]

After drawing a clear connection between the progressive
income tax and communism ("a graduated income tax is one of
the principles of Karl Marx' [pronunciation guide omitted]
Communist Manifesto"), one School of Tomorrow/Accelerated
Christian Education American history booklet for high school
students issues a call to reform or abolish the progressive income
tax, which "*penalize*[s]" workers with higher incomes, by stating
that "it was wrong for outlaw Robin Hood to steal from the rich
and give to the poor, and it is wrong for governments to do it. The
U.S. tax laws need to be changed."[123] The booklet makes the con-

nection between Robin Hood and the socialism inherent in the progressive income tax in a preceding paragraph:

> A graduated income tax is not equitable because it penalizes those who, through diligent hard work and self-discipline, earn more money. Part of the money from these higher taxes is used to fund government giveaway programs, such as food stamps, which are sometimes given even to those who refuse to work. Taking from the rich to give to the poor is one of the basic principles of socialism. Robin Hood [pronunciation guide omitted] an *outlaw* of English legend robbed from the rich to give to the poor. To many people Robin Hood is a hero; but, in fact he was just a thief.[124]

The Treatment of Government Issues

Appearing almost concurrently with the explicit and strongly expressed advocacy of a free-market economy are discussions of the proper role of the federal government and issues related to federalism. Local and state governments are less objectionable than the federal government. For example, state judges are treated in relatively neutral fashion while federal judges are frequently accused of subverting the intent of the Founders by basing their jurisprudence on their personal liberal views.

In a different vein, the texts mix constitutional and political arguments in favor of both limited and reduced federal power and jurisdiction. For example, a subsection of the "Federalism" chapter in A Beka's civics textbook is titled "Gutting the Tenth Amendment"[125] In a second subsection, titled "Preemptions," the authors state that "the most intrusive application of preemption has been in the Clean Air Act of 1970."[126] The Motor Voter Law of 1993 is described as a "controversial . . . unfunded mandate."[127] The chapter, devoted to the executive branch of government, includes a highlighted text box more than two pages long that consists of material adapted from "Petty Dictatorships Are Proliferating in the Federal Government," a chapter from a book by James Bovard.[128] Bovard argues that the Food and Drug

Administration and the Environmental Protection Agency are engaging in a "reign of terror."[129] Another highlighted text box in the same chapter quotes a *Pensacola News Journal* article titled "The Danger of an Almighty Bureaucracy."[130] Bob Jones' civics textbook asks students, "What factors have rendered the Tenth Amendment ineffective?"[131] Teachers are told that students will have varied answers, but they are also told that "the courts have reinterpreted this amendment in such a way as to alter its original intent and to render it ineffective. The federal government has not crusaded for increased states' rights because such rights would restrict many of the broad powers that the federal government has accrued."[132]

Some of the harshest language in all three publishers' materials is directed at the federal judiciary, which is blamed for expanding federal authority, encouraging discrimination against Christians, and contributing to a variety of social ills. Federal judges have substituted their own "personal values" and "prejudices" for the intent of the Founders.[133] In discussing how courts interpret the Constitution, the textbooks juxtapose such terms as "judicial activism" and "judicial restraint" or "strict construction" and "loose construction." In addition, both Bob Jones and A Beka textbooks routinely label individual Supreme Court justices as "liberal" or "conservative."

The nature of the coverage received by the justices and by a number of Supreme Court decisions corresponds to whether the justices' opinions would be acceptable to conservatives.[134] A School of Tomorrow/Accelerated Christian Education booklet links humanism and the *Roe* v. *Wade* decision with criticism of the doctrine of judicial review:

> The decision, an illustration of un-Godly, humanistic reasoning was all too similar to [the *Dred Scott* decision] . . . These decisions [*Roe* and *Dred Scott*] of the Supreme Court went far beyond the authority granted it by the Constitution. The justices, who were not elected to office, have given themselves the power to make law on their own by ruling on the legality of laws made by the U.S. Congress

and state legislatures. The Constitution gave the Supreme Court power only to settle disputes on the basis of the Constitution, the laws of the United States, and treaties.[135]

The booklet does not mention that the principle of judicial review was established by *Marbury* v. *Madison* in 1803. Nor does it discuss how the Court would "settle disputes" without interpreting the Constitution itself, especially when a litigant challenges the constitutionality of a law or government policy or practice.

A Beka's civics book criticizes the 14th Amendment and, by extension, the process of incorporation that made the Bill of Rights apply to state governments, and thus emphasizes the negative rather than the positive effects of this development on constitutional jurisprudence. The following passage from A Beka's American government textbook exemplifies this view the of 14th Amendment:

> This amendment is *the source of federal civil rights legislation*. In many cases, however, Congress has not made use of this power but has allowed the Supreme Court to dictate law under Section 1 [requiring due process before states can deprive individuals of life, liberty, or property] of this amendment. Through the use of this amendment, the Court has abridged the rights of the states and of individual citizens.[136]

This view is echoed in Bob Jones' civics textbook. Given the highly negative stance toward gays and gay rights, the author consigns the amendment to guilt by association with "evils," such as gays and gay rights, that are contrary to God's will:

> The activist Warren Court [in striking the separate but equal doctrine of *Plessy* v. *Ferguson*], however, was not hampered by constitutional wording, nor patient for congressional action legislation. Giving the XIV Amendment a broad social interpretation, the high court struck down the Kansas law [prohibiting black and white children from attending the same school] and paved the way for courts nationwide to extend these newly discovered rights to everything from housing to homosexuality.[137]

Bob Jones' high school U.S. history book also addresses the 14th Amendment and the process of incorporation in several passages. When discussing the drafting of the Constitution, the authors opine that "[n]ot until the 20th century did the Supreme Court place most of the Bill of Rights restrictions on the states, in an effort to expand national authority."[138] They also describe the 14th Amendment as having "eventually be[come] a wedge that the central government used to enter and eventually control many state and local affairs."[139] The authors state that "in a typical example of judicial activism . . ." the Supreme Court justices applied the "equal protection of the law" clause of the 14th Amendment to its voter rights and redistricting decisions.[140]

The textbooks demonstrate a distaste for political process based on democratic, as opposed to republican, principles. Most contemporary Americans do not appear to find the direct election of senators a cause for concern. Yet Bob Jones' U.S. history textbook criticizes the passage of the 17th Amendment with this statement: "By replacing republicanism with increased democratization, however, the amendment also eliminated one of the safeguards which the Founding Fathers had so painstakingly built into our federal system of government."[141] The comparable text from A Beka makes a similar point, albeit less directly: "This amendment *provided for the direct election of senators by the voters of a state* (rather than by the state legislature as planned in the Constitution)."[142] A U.S. history booklet from School of Tomorrow/Accelerated Christian Education describes the effect of the 17th Amendment as "destroy[ing] this balance [between the states and the federal government] of power. Congress was changed. . . to a unicameral (one house) system that represents only the people's interests. States rights were weakened, and the growth of a powerful central government was encouraged."[143] The authors' view of the 17th Amendment is entirely consistent not only with the text's disdain for the federal government but also with their distrust of direct democratic processes generally.

The Treatment of Foreign Affairs

Like the School of Tomorrow/Accelerated Christian Education booklets described by Fleming and Hunt in 1987, both the company's more recent materials and the textbooks from Bob Jones and A Beka devote a great deal of space to the issue of communism. While virtually all government intervention in the economic sphere is described in negative terms, the coverage of communism and socialism is distinguished by its depth, frequency, and extreme hostility. What Fleming and Hunt describe as "an almost paranoid fear of the Communist conspiracy in all aspects of modern life" pervades the materials from all three publishers.[144] From the standpoint of these textbooks, the dangers of communism and socialism and the struggle against them are the driving forces of the postwar era. The end of the Cold War does not seem to have affected their stance toward communism and socialism. The authors' rhetoric can best be described as passionate, and their depth of feeling is matched only in their more abbreviated discussions of abortion, prayer in the schools, the dangers of religious and political liberalism, and so on. They also express a substantial degree of animosity toward the United Nations. The A Beka high school world history text contains some of the harshest language:

> Contrary to the basic Judeo-Christian concept of law which places limits on government, the UN charter laid the foundation for one-world government with unlimited power. . . . The UN founders envisioned an all-powerful, global authority with power to bend nations into conformity with its plans for the "world community." Given the radical agenda and the totalitarian philosophy of the UN, one can quickly discern the threat of its plan for world government to the political, religious, and social liberty of all free peoples. It is a collectivist juggernaut that would crush individual freedom and force the will of an elite few on all of humanity.[145]

Foreign aid cannot solve international problems because in many instances the cause of economic problems and political instability lies in the spiritual realm. President "Kennedy believed that poverty made [the countries of Latin America] vulnerable to communism [but] foreign aid could not solve the spiritual problems that lay at the root of Latin America's economic and political difficulties."[146]

Fleming and Hunt note only one major inconsistency in the School of Tomorrow/Accelerated Christian Education materials they studied: the treatment of the United Nations as both a worthy and effective organization and one whose actions have led to the expansion of communism. I found the same inconsistency. Perhaps it can be traced to a distinct element of determinism and fatalism regarding both the UN and other human attempts to influence international problems, including efforts to promote peace. For example, A Beka's ninth-grade world history textbook opines pessimistically that "the organizers of the UN did not realize that international war and unrest cannot be eradicated from a world filled with men possessing a sinful, selfish nature."[147] Bob Jones' current events textbook states that "the troubles in the Balkans continually remind Christians about the inability of men to solve their own problems. International efforts to bring peace have only worsened the problems."[148] The text continues, "Only the King of Kings will be able to bring all nations together when he returns."[149] Similarly, the publisher's high school American history book discounts efforts to achieve peace through diplomacy:

> The search for lasting peace in the world is elusive given the fact that troubled areas reflect troubled hearts. Injustice, hatred, greed, cruelty are as prevalent as the sinful hearts from which those actions and attitudes proceed. Man's nature ensures that peace on a world-wide scale will never be permanent until Christ returns. However, on an individual level, peace is available through the Prince of Peace — by accepting Jesus Christ as Savior and Lord. Making peace between warring nations is commendable and there is no shortage of work, but the solutions are often temporary. Only Christ can provide the peace that is lasting and satisfying.[150]

The influence of predestination is plain and perhaps reaches its apogee in Bob Jones' civics text:

> In spite of who sits in the White House or who rules in the Kremlin, or how many treaties or hydrogen bombs are pro-duced, God is still on the throne, and our confidence is in Him. No one will accidentally "push the button" that destroys the world. God remains in control and His timetable for the world will not have to be hastily rewritten.[151]

One interesting lens through which this worldview can be examined is that of metaphorical analysis. Lakoff assigns a series of metaphors to conservative and liberal positions.[152] Conserva-tives order their world according to a Strict Father morality while liberals embrace an ethos based on the idea of the Nurturant Parent. When both groups see government as parent, they apply either Strict Father or Nurturant Parent morality to their concep-tion of its proper role. Although I cannot do justice to Lakoff's analysis in the context of this discussion, what he observes about the Strict Father metaphor is highly relevant to civic education found in Christian school textbooks. Strict Father morality is grounded in the nuclear family, with the father having responsi-bility for setting boundaries on behavior through the use of pun-ishments and rewards, while the mother is the nurturing parent. Strict Father morality is necessary because the family and, by extension, the state or society in general is besieged by evil by forces that lead to anarchy and chaos.

Strict Father morality is a meritocractic hierarchy, in other words, a moral order in which God is dominant and has moral authority over all people. Human beings have dominion or moral authority over the natural world, adults over children, and men over women. That which challenges the moral order is wrong and immoral. Small wonder, then, that textbooks so strongly based on conservative ideology give short shrift to the suffering of African Americans under slavery and the arguments of the abolitionist movement. The civil rights movement, likewise, represents a fail-ure to conform to the prevailing moral order of the times and thus, unlike abortion, evokes no impassioned rhetoric. The authors of these texts depict both homosexuality and abortion as great evils. "Homosexuality challenges the very idea that the Strict Father family is the right model of the family and therefore of morality and politics."[153] Likewise, abortion also challenges the very foundations of Strict Father morality. Women's roles are viewed as subordinate. For a woman to chose an abortion is for her to place her self-interest above that of the family. Under the Moral Order metaphor in the Strict Father schema, "women should not be choosing careers or an independent careerist life-style above their natural role as mothers in a family. When she chooses abortion over motherhood, she is violating the moral order and challenging the entire Strict Family morality."[154] In addition, unmarried sex is viewed as moral weakness because it also challenges the proper structure of the family.

The Morality of Reward and Punishment is another dominant metaphor because, in a world in which survival is paramount, people must learn to compete successfully. The self-discipline that leads to successful competition allows us to identify those who are moral. In Lakoff's words, "Rewards given to those who have not deserved them through competition are immoral. They remove the need for self-discipline and they remove the need for obedience to authority."[155] Christian school textbooks consistently emphasize the need for individual responsibility and decry government interventions that would ameliorate the consequences of competing unsuccessfully. Even as adult children are set free to "sink or swim" and "good parents do not meddle or interfere in their lives," so, too, government should not meddle in the lives of its citizens.[156]

The textbooks' views on poverty, both in their discussions of the progressive and social gospel movements as responses to the Industrial Revolution and more recent antipoverty programs, such as Social Security, conform to Lakoff's Morality of Rewards and Punishments. Structural causes of and solutions for poverty are discounted, and stress is placed on the moral weakness of individuals. Social programs are inherently unnatural and immoral. Socialism and communism are government systems that discourage individual incentive and self-discipline and encourage laziness and moral weakness. Taxes, because they redistribute wealth, tend to undercut the competition that flows naturally from a free-market system, thus diminishing the rewards for self-discipline. What is particularly odd about these views of competition, disparities in wealth, and the conservative animosity toward efforts to ameliorate these inequities is that applying the theological doctrine of "innate depravity" to economic well-being bears more than a passing resemblance to social Darwinism. Those who have the "right stuff" will succeed, and those who fail should not be helped lest society reward their moral failings, such as lack of self-discipline.

Lakoff's dissection of the Strict Father morality makes it clear why conservatives generally and conservative families in particular regard the inculcation of their values as a moral issue and why the failure of the public schools to foster the development of Strict Father morality compels them to seek alternative education for their children. But believing that Strict Father morality is necessary for the nation's well-being also provides impetus to make this type of education more widely available for others.

The discussion in this chapter goes a long way toward answering the question of why many conservative organizations advocate various programs that have as a goal the partial or complete privatization of American education. At the deepest level, conservatives and conservative organizations are true believers in Strict Father morality. Few conservative foundations (including those heavily involved in the current voucher and tuition tax credit movements), conservative commentators, or conservative leaders would disavow the opinions conveyed to children and adolescents by these textbooks. Indeed, one of the primary reasons, if not *the* primary reason, for their support of vouchers and various school choice programs is to expose larger numbers of American students to conservative ideology.

Notes

1. Dan B. Fleming and Thomas C. Hunt, "The World as Seen by Students in Accelerated Christian Education Schools," *Phi Delta Kappan* 68 (March 1987): 523.

2. Kurt S. Grussendorf, Michael R. Lowman, and Brian S. Ashbaugh, *America: Land That I Love, Teacher Edition* (Pensacola, Fla.: A Beka Books, 1994), p. 481.

3. Timothy Keesee, *American Government for Christian Schools, Teacher's Edition* (Greenville, S.C.: Bob Jones University Press, 1998), p. 138.

4. Jerry H. Combee, *History of the World in Christian Perspective, Teacher Edition*, 3rd ed. (Pensacola, Fla.: A Beka Books, 1995), p. 440.

5. Grussendorf, Lowman, and Ashbaugh, op. cit., p. 465.

6. George Thompson and Jerry Combee, *World History and Cultures in Christian Perspective*, 2nd ed. (Pensacola, Fla: A Beka, 1997), p. 446.

7. Ibid., p. 445.

8. Ibid.

9. Ibid.

10. Ibid.

11. *Social Studies, U.S. Civics-4* (#1137) (n.p. : Accelerated Christian Education, 1997), p. 21.

12. *The History of Our United States, Teacher Edition*, 2nd ed. (Pensacola, Fla.: A Beka Books, 1994), p. 297.

13. "One great example of African-American achievement was the appointment of Justice Clarence Thomas to the Supreme Court by President Bush. Thomas had been born to poor sharecroppers in the hills of Georgia. Through his own hard work and God-given ability, he earned a law degree and achieved several important government positions, including assistant attorney general for Missouri and judge for the U.S. Court of Appeals for the District of Columbia." *The History of Our United States*, p. 297. The publisher's eighth-grade U.S. history book gives Thurgood Marshall six lines: "President Johnson . . . appointed the first black Associate Justice of the Supreme Court, Thurgood Marshall. As a young lawyer Marshall had argued the 1954 *Brown* vs. *the Board of Education* case before the Supreme Court" (Grussendorf, Low-

man, Ashbaugh, op. cit., p. 473). While Thomas is not given the effusive treatment of the fourth-grade text, Grussendorf, Lowman, and Ashbaugh do give him two more lines of text than Marshall and again a color photograph (p. 505). The publisher's high school American history text gives Marshall three lines of text (the first sentence of the eighth-grade text's two statements about Marshall) and a color photograph but gives eight lines and a color photograph to Thomas. Michael Lowman, George Thompson, and Kurt Grussendorf, *United States History in Christian Perspective: Heritage of Freedom*, 2nd ed. (Pensacola, Fla.: A Beka, 1996), pp. 631, 669. The photograph of Marshall is captioned "Thurgood Marshall," while that of Thomas is captioned "Justice Clarence Thomas" (Lowman, Thompson, and Grussendorf, pp. 631, 669). Both texts use virtually identical language when discussing Thomas' nomination: "In 1991, President Bush nominated federal judge Clarence Thomas to the Supreme Court to replace the retiring Thurgood Marshall. Many liberals opposed Thomas's appointment because of his conservative views, but after much debate the Senate confirmed his appointment to the Court" (Lowman, Thompson, and Grussendorf, p. 669). The eighth-grade book merely omits the "but" to make two sentences. (Grussendorf, Lowman, and Ashbaugh, p. 505).
14. Keesee, op. cit., p. 31.
15. "Which Way, America? 1980-1994: The Reagan Era and the '90s," in Grussendorf, Lowman, and Ashbaugh, op. cit., pp. 490-512.
16. Combee, op. cit., p. 469.
17. Keesee, op. cit., p. 184.
18. *The American Republic for Christian Schools, Teachers Edition* (Greenville, S.C: Bob Jones University Press, 1988), p. 451.
19. *The American Republic for Christian Schools*, p. 516.
20. William R. Bowen et al., *American Government in Christian Perspective*, 2nd ed. (Pensacola, Fla.: A Beka, 1997), p. 19.
21. Ibid.
22. Ibid.
23. Keesee, op. cit., p. 6.
24. Bowen et al., op. cit., p. 17. The Bob Jones' text posits the beginning of this need for government after the Flood "as a means of controlling the kind of violence that had consumed the antediluvian world" (Keesee, op. cit., p. 6).

25. Bowen et al., op. cit., p. 19.

26. *Heritage Studies 4 for Christian Schools: Doors of Opportunity, Nineteenth Century America, Teacher's Edition* (Greenville, S.C.: Bob Jones University Press, 1997), p. 247. Student edition, p. 187.

27. *Heritage Studies 4*, p. 246. In addition, the teacher's notes state that "Christians living in socialist countries suffer also from lack of religious freedom" (p. 246).

28. Bowen et al., op. cit., p. 22, 23.

29. Ibid., p. 29-31.

30. Ibid., p. 31.

31. Keesee, op. cit., p. 383.

32. Ibid., p. 384.

33. Ibid., p. 385-86. "Qualities such as initiative, personal responsibility, and personal reward are clearly valued in this parable. The economic system that best permits freedom and personal accountability is capitalism. A command system [all forms of socialism, including European mixed economies] diminishes these characteristics by placing responsibility upon an overarching state and not upon the individual. Clearly, capitalism [which is at odds with socialism] is the better system — the economic partner of political liberty" (p. 386).

34. *Colonial Period*. Self-Pac® of Basic Education (#110), rev. 1995. (n.p.: Reform Publications, 1974), p. 17.

35. *World History Between 1850 and 1950*. Self-Pac® of Basic Education (#106), rev. 1995 (n.p.: Reform Publications, 1974), p. 4. In the opinion of the booklet's author, "The capitalists reformed many of the harsh conditions that existed in factories" (p. 4).

36. Ibid.

37. Ibid., p. 5.

38. Ibid.

39. Thompson and Combee, op. cit., p. 513. This statement is immediately followed by a discussion of diminution of the nation's "Christian heritage [as] the seeds of materialism and liberalism that had been planted by intellectual leaders in the first half of the century began to take root" (p. 513).

40. Timothy Keesee and Mark Sidwell, *United States History for Christian Schools, Teacher's Edition*. 2nd ed. (Pensacola, Fla.: A Beka, 1991), p. 551. A Beka's senior high school history text con-

tains a similar view of McCarthy. Although the authors note that "his critics pointed out that McCarthy's methods were not always the wisest," they opine that "many of [his] conclusions, although technically unprovable, were drawn from the accumulation of undisputed facts." Lowman, Thompson, and Grussendorf, op. cit., pp. 593-94.

41. Keesee and Sidwell, op. cit., p. 551.

42. Ibid., p. 605. They continue by describing the Equal Rights Amendment as "the most controversial and divisive piece of pro-feminist legislation" and attribute its existence to the efforts of "radicals" (p. 606).

43. Grussendorf, Lowman, and Ashbaugh, op. cit., p. 492.

44. Lowman, Thompson, and Grussendorf, op. cit., p. 652.

45. Grussendorf, Lowman, and Ashbaugh, op. cit., p. 492.

46. *Social Studies 1096*, rev. 1998 (n.p.: Accelerated Christian Education, 1990), p. 26.

47. Lowman, Thompson, and Grussendorf, op. cit., p. 651.

48. *Teacher's Resource Guide to Current Events for Christian Schools, 1998-1999* (Greenville, S.C.: Bob Jones University Press, 1998), p. 65.

49. *The History of Our United States*, p. 307.

50. Grussendorf, Lowman, and Ashbaugh, op. cit., p. 506.

51. Ibid., p. 506-507.

52. *Social Studies 1094*, rev. 1998 (n.p.: Accelerated Christian Education, 1990), p. 6. This point is reinforced by a review question in which the term "socialistic philosophy" is to be matched with its definition, "the basis of President Roosevelt's programs" (p. 1).

53. *Social Studies 1093*, rev. 1998 (n.p.: Accelerated Christian Education, 1990), p. 31. This statement is reinforced by being included as one the self-test questions for the booklet.

54. Keesee and Sidwell, op. cit., p. 500.

55. Lowman, Thompson, and Grussendorf et al., op. cit., p. 597.

56. *Social Studies 1095*, rev. 1998 (n.p.: Accelerated Christian Education, 1990), p. 9.

57. Grussendorf, Lowman, and Ashbaugh, op. cit., p. 465.

58. Ibid., p. 467.

59. Ibid., p. 465.

60. Lowman, Thompson, and Grussendorf, op. cit., p. 630. "Well-intentioned civil rights reforms" had negative consequences such

as "funds for urban housing [being] wasted on deals between con-
tractors and big city bosses" and "many people . . . not tak[ing]
care of the property they were given by the government because
they did not have to work for it" (p. 630). Overall, there is very little praise for the civil rights movement in this section and an
emphasis on its negative aspects. Both black and white
Southerners "resented" these intrusions into their way of life.
"Segregation had become an accepted way of life . . ." (p. 630).
Although resentment led to some becoming extremists, the Klu
Klux Klan is mentioned once while the authors devote 17 lines to
"black separatist groups" (p. 631).

61. Keesee and Sidwell, op. cit., pp. 606, 620.

62. Ibid., p. 288.

63. *Social Studies.* Self-Pac® of Basic Education (#107), rev. 1997
    (n.p.: School of Tomorrow, 1974), p. 33. The coverage of President
    Clinton contrasts with that given to Watergate. Although the book-
    let states clearly that "taped telephone conversations . . . proved
    conclusively that wrongdoing was widespread from the President
    down," it makes a number of statements that undercut any con-
    demnation of the scandal (p. 32). For example, "Of course, this
    type of activity has happened before to both the Republican and
    Democratic parties. The question for future historians is whether
    Watergate would have ever been the national issue it became if the
    news media had not greatly 'played-up' the event" (p. 32). It
    should be noted that similar statements are not made when the
    booklets discuss scandals associated with the Clinton presidency.

64. Grussendorf, Lowman, and Ashbaugh, op. cit., p. 506.

65. Keesee, op. cit., p. 22.

66. *The American Republic for Christian Schools*, pp. 610-11.

67. Thompson and Combee, op. cit., p. 513.

68. Ibid.

69. *The History of Our United States*, p. 302.

70. Bowen et al., op. cit., p. 16.

71. Keesee, op. cit., p. 5. The author makes clear, however, that the
    wife is not an "inferior" but a "companion and helper" (p. 5).

72. Ibid.

73. *The American Republic for Christian Schools*, p. 610.

74. *The Post-World War II Period.* Self-Pac® of Basic Education
    (#120) (n.p.: School of Tomorrow, 1998), p. 44. This discussion
    occurs in a section titled "Responding to Moral Decay" (p. 44).

75. Ibid. The booklet includes Louis Farrakhan and the Million Man March as one of the "religious organizations that are more successful at providing solutions" (although "secular organizations are quick to identify problems in society") but does not explicitly mention the Nation of Islam.

76. Ibid. Berlet and Lyons describe the organization as exemplifying "soft dominionism and apocalyptic scapegoating." Chip Berlet and Matthew N. Lyons, *Right-Wing Populism in America: Too Close for Comfort* (New York: Guilford, 2000), p. 328.

77. *The History of Our United States*, pp. 299, 320.

78. *The American Republic for Christian Schools*, p. 610. Other examples of this breakdown include "the elimination of dress codes in most schools" and the cohabitation of unmarried couples (p. 610).

79. *The Post-World War II Period*, p. 37.

80. Ibid.

81. *The History of Our United States*, p. 299.

82. *The American Republic for Christian Schools*, p. 599.

83. Bowen et al., op. cit., p. 151.

84. Keesee, op. cit., p. 292. See also Chapter 3.

85. *Social Studies 1096*, pp. 6-7. Durham notes the linkage between abortion and the Holocaust. See Martin Durham, *The Christian Right, the Far Right, and the Boundaries of American Conservatism* (Manchester, England, and New York: Manchester University Press, 2000), p. 86.

86. *Teacher's Resource Guide to Current Events*, p. 21.

87. Keesee, op. cit., p. 138.

88. *The American Republic for Christian Schools*, p. 609.

89. Lowman, Thompson, and Grussendorf, op. cit., p. 631.

90. Keesee and Sidwell, op. cit., p. 269.

91. Ibid., p. 219.

92. Lowman, Thompson, and Grussendorf, op. cit., p. 219.

93. *Teacher's Resource Guide to Current Events*, p. 34.

94. Keesee and Sidwell, op. cit., pp. 478-79.

95. Ibid., p. 479.

96. *The American Republic for Christian Schools*, p. 373.

97. *Social Studies 1091*, rev. 1998 (n.p.: Accelerated Christian Education, 1990), p. 11.

98. Bowen et al., op. cit., p. 17.

99. Ibid., p. 17.

100. Ibid., p. 36, quoting Robert L. Moyer, "Shall a Christian Obey Human Governors," in *The Sword Book of Treasures,* edited by John R. Rice (Murfreesboro, Tenn.: Sword of the Lord, 1946), pp. 90-92.

101. *Approaching the Twenty-First Century*, Self-Pac® of Basic Education (#108) (n.p.: School of Tomorrow, 1996), p. 16. The booklet asserts that, though "more Americans attended church in a single week than attended all professional football, basketball, and baseball games during an entire year. . . . In other nations, especially in the Third World, the number of believers is increasing at a much more rapid rate" than in Canada and the United States (p. 16).

102. *The Post-World War II Period, Social Studies*, p. 44.

103. "As opponents of the government school system argued in 1800s, if you remove Christianity from the schools, then inevitably it will be replaced by the state religion of secular humanism. History has proven them correct." Charley Reese, "Education Defined by Content," *Valdosta* (Georgia) *Daily Times*, 16 May 2001, p. 6A.

104. *Social Studies 1093*, p. 5.

105. Lowman, Thompson, and Grussendorf, op. cit., pp. 673. Note the similarity to a statement in Eagle Forum's *Phyllis Schlafly Report*: "Since schools receive additional federal money for every child labeled learning disabled, there is a financial incentive to increase the numbers." "Dumbing Down and Developing Diversity," *Phyllis Schlafly Report* (March 2001): 1.

106. *Social Studies, U.S. Civics-4* (#1136), p. 15.

107. One of the clearest examples of this attribution of misfortune to personal failings occurs in a review of *PC, M.D.* by Sally Satel, written by a conservative columnist. Taking issue with a statement in an *American Journal for Public Health* that called on its readers to address social inequalities that lead to inequalities in health, Satel, as repeated by Hart, asserts that "for a variety of non-economic reasons poorer people are more likely than their more affluent peers to be obese, to lead a sedentary lifestyle, and to engage in various kinds of risky behaviors." Betsy Hart, "Politically Correct Medicine," *Valdosta Daily Times*, 16 April

2001, p. 6A. The medical establishment, according to Satel, ignores these causes of poor health in a "pursuit of more politically correct answers" (p. 6A).

108. *The Turn of the Century, 1890-1914, Social Studies*, Self-Pac® of Basic Education (#118) (n.p.: School of Tomorrow, 1998), p. 38.

109. *Social Studies 1094*, p. 6.

110. Ibid.

111. Ibid.

112. Ibid., p. 7.

113. Keesee, op. cit., pp. 403-404.

114. Ibid., p. 405. The author notes that this good incentive also conforms with the Bible: "Ephesians 6:5-7 admonishes workers to have this diligence (not necessarily for fear of losing their jobs, but to please the Lord)" (p. 405).

115. Grussendorf, Lowman, and Ashbaugh, op. cit., p. 467. Presumably those who take advantage of welfare benefits also take advantage of "working citizens" whose taxes fund government welfare programs, as the following paragraph points out (p. 467). The text goes on to note that such "programs increas[ed] the influence of liberal politicians" and led to "false prosperity" because government was "living beyond its means and borrowing large amounts of money" (p. 467). A few pages later the authors do not mention the Reagan deficits except to describe them as inherited from the Carter Administration and as a result of the failure of Congress "to discipline its spending" (pp. 493-94).

116. Lowman, Thompson, and Grussendorf, op. cit., p. 656.

117. Ibid.

118. Grussendorf, Lowman, and Ashbaugh, op. cit., p. 507.

119. Keesee, op. cit., p. 391.

120. Ibid., p. 386.

121. Keesee and Sidwell, op. cit., p. 420.

122. Ibid.

123. *Social Studies 1093*, pp. 6-7. The word *penalized* is printed in red ink as a vocabulary word.

124. Ibid., p. 6. The word *outlaw* is printed in red ink as vocabulary word.

125. Bowen et al., op. cit., p. 185.

126. Ibid.

127. Ibid., p. 186.

128. Ibid., pp. 135-37. The source cited is James Bovard, *Lost Rights: The Destruction of American Liberty* (New York: St. Martin's Press, 1994). No page numbers are given.

129. Ibid., p. 136.

130. Ibid., p. 131.

131. Keesee, op. cit., p. 117.

132. Ibid., p. 119.

133. *Social Studies, U.S. Civics-4* (#1136), p. 29; and *Social Studies, U.S. Civics-2*, p. 31.

134. See generally, Chapter Three.

135. *Social Studies 1096*, p. 6.

136. Bowen et al., op. cit., p. 169.

137. Keesee, op. cit., p. 291. This discussion is accompanied by an Oliphant cartoon that shows the justices spoon-feeding "love and understanding" to a defendant who is holding a gun. The cartoon caption reads, "Come now there is no such thing as a bad boy . . ." The caption in the book states that "decisions made by liberal activists in the courts have weakened law enforcement in recent years." It is obviously placed to accompany the subsequent discussion of criminal law, which begins, "Law enforcement is an area that has been weakened by liberal activists on the court" (p. 291).

138. Keesee and Sidwell, op. cit., p. 155. Some might argue that the process of incorporation was undertaken to protect the rights of individual citizens against the excesses of state government, but this view is not presented. The process of incorporation led to an expansion of "national authority," but that does not necessarily make it the purpose of making the Bill of Rights apply to the states.

139. Keesee and Sidwell, op. cit., p. 348. The authors lament that "today the American citizen usually cannot avoid contact — even conflict — with the national bureaucracy" (p. 348). The full passage reads:

> The Fourteenth Amendment, as mentioned earlier, eventually became a wedge that the central government used to enter and eventually control many state and local affairs.

> One historian noted that before the Civil War virtually the only agency of the national government that touched the lives of the average citizen was the Post Office. Today, the American citizen usually cannot avoid contact — even conflict — with the national bureaucracy. (p. 348)

140. Ibid., p. 567. The authors indicate their displeasure with the decisions of the Warren Court by quoting Justice Harlan's dissent in *Reynolds* v *Sims*, 377 U.S. 533 (1964), followed by this sentence: "Unfortunately, the majority of Harlan's associates did not listen to him" (p. 567).
141. Ibid., p. 420.
142. Bowen et al., op. cit., p. 169.
143. *Social Studies 1093*, p. 7.
144. Fleming and Hunt, op. cit., p. 523.
145. Thompson and Combee, op. cit., p. 573.
146. Grussendorf, Lowman, and Ashbaugh, op. cit., pp. 465-66.
147. Combee, op. cit., p. 490.
148. *Teacher's Resource Guide to Current Events*, p. 108.
149. Ibid.
150. Keesee, op. cit., p. 315.
151. Ibid., p. 334.
152. George Lakoff, *Moral Politics: What Conservatives Know that Liberals Don't* (Chicago: University of Chicago Press, 1996).
153. Ibid., p. 225.
154. Ibid., p. 268.
155. Ibid., p. 68.
156. Ibid., pp. 66-67.

CHAPTER THREE

"Give Me That Ol' Time Constitution"[1]

Having a citizenry that is well educated regarding the role of law in our society is a highly desirable goal. In this chapter I examine the views of the law that are presented to many Christian school students by analyzing how the textbooks used by these students treat the constitutional jurisprudence of the Supreme Court. As in Chapter Two, the focus is on civics and American history textbooks and related materials. Eight textbooks, including five U.S. history texts, two high school civics texts, and one current events text from A Beka Books and Bob Jones University Press form the foundation for this discussion. In addition, I examined 18 School of Tomorrow/Accelerated Christian Education booklets, including 12 high school U.S. history booklets and 6 civics/American government booklets.[2]

General Characteristics

One of the overarching characteristics of textbooks used in Christian schools is the juxtaposition of factual and editorial material. This pedagogical approach is particularly apparent in the selection and treatment of Supreme Court cases and constitutional law issues. Many cases appear to be selected to support a conservative religious-political viewpoint, rather than to teach about the law per se. However, because the subject matter of the cases also reflects major issues in American constitutional jurisprudence, the mere inclusion of cases is not, by itself, sufficient to support the assertion that the coverage reflects an intentional use of the texts to persuade, rather than to inform. The amount of coverage given to the selected cases also must be considered. Some simple comparisons are instructive. The only two cases that are included in each of the eight textbooks and at least one School of Tomorrow booklet are *Brown* v. *Board of Education* and *Roe* v. *Wade*. Twenty-three religion cases are discussed or mentioned 59 times, whereas two desegregation cases, the *Brown* case and *Swann* v. *Charlotte-Mecklenburg Board of Education*, are discussed or mentioned 14 times, and nine historical cases are discussed 39 times. Thus the number of religion cases is more than double the number of cases related to civil rights and cases of historical importance, and the religion cases are more likely to be discussed or mentioned than are cases in both of these categories combined.

Selection and coverage alone cannot convey the persuasive character of the books' approach to constitutional law. Indeed, a neutral presentation could be based on these cases if the treatment attempted to convey a balanced discussion of the issues involved. How the cases are presented is crucial to understanding the view of the Constitution and the judicial system that these texts present. Both explicit and implicit bias are present. For example, the authors use slanted language to disparage, either subtly or sharply, the reasoning of the Court when they disagree with a particular decision. For example, Bob Jones' civics book employs sarcasm when describing the citation of *Griswold* in *Roe* as "the so-called right to privacy which had been recently 'discovered'."[3]

In addition, the authors structure their discussions of cases and their associated legal issues to shape students' beliefs and perceptions. They use four methods to attempt to influence student thinking. First, the authors do not present both sides of the legal arguments. This omission is most noticeable when the coverage of the issue is extensive and the issue is one that is of concern to religious-political conservatives, for example, abortion or school prayer. They also fail to include the reasoning of the Court in reaching its decision. Second, the authors focus on what they consider negative social results that flowed from the decision. Expository material describing the social consequences of Supreme Court decisions is included only when the case deals with a conservative issue of concern. Thus the consequences of *Plessy* are not described while those of *Roe* are addressed in every textbook. Third, they include editorial comments to reinforce the conservative ideology presented. Again, this occurs only when the case deals with an issue about which conservatives have strong opinions. Fourth, the inclusion of quotations from dissenting opinions also follows this general pattern. In some instances a quote from a majority opinion is balanced by a quote from a dissenting opinion. In other instances a holding statement is given together with a quote from a dissent. However, the decision to include quotations from dissenting opinions appears to be made not for its efficacy in illustrating how lawyers and judges can disagree over a legal point, but for its ideological value.

The cases discussed in these textbooks can be grouped into five categories:

- Historical cases.[4]
- First Amendment cases (24 religion cases, 14 freedom of speech cases, and four freedom of assembly cases).
- Abortion cases.
- Public school desegregation cases.
- Miscellaneous cases (five criminal law cases, two civil rights cases, two apportionment cases, and several others, including *Jones* v. *Clinton*[5] and *Griswold* v. *Connecticut*[6]).

Not unexpectedly, the civics textbooks included more cases than the American history books, and high school textbooks included more cases than elementary and junior high school or middle grades books.

The most frequently discussed cases were *Brown* v. *Board of Education*[7] (discussed or mentioned 12 times and appearing in nine books or booklets), *Roe* v. *Wade*[8] (discussed or mentioned 10 times and appearing in nine books or booklets), *Marbury* v. *Madison*[9] (discussed or mentioned seven times in seven books), *Engel* v. *Vitale*[10] (discussed or mentioned seven times and appearing in seven books or booklets), *Plessy* v. Ferguson[11] (discussed or mentioned six times in six books or booklets), and *Abington School District* v. *Schempp*[12] (discussed or mentioned six times in four books or booklets).

Historical Cases

Historical cases discussed or mentioned in these textbooks include *Marbury* v. *Madison, McCulloch* v. *Maryland, Trustees of Dartmouth College* v. *Woodward, Gibbons* v. *Ogden, Dred Scott* v. *Sandford, Plessy* v. *Ferguson, Panama Refining Company* v. *Ryan* (National Industrial Recovery Act declared an unconstitutional delegation of legislative power to the executive branch), *United States* v. *Butler* (Agricultural Adjustment Act declared unconstitutional because the General Welfare clause merely allows Congress the power to appropriate tax revenue for the general welfare), and *Northern Securities* v. *United States* (formation of a railroad stock holding company was a violation of the Sherman Antitrust Act).[13] For the most part, the discussion of these cases is neutral, though slightly tilted toward a negative opinion regarding judicial review and of the federal government as opposed to state governments. Negative or critical remarks toward these historical cases, when included, are relatively mild when compared to the treatment given other types of cases, such as abortion, religion, freedom of speech, and death penalty cases.

The treatment of *Marbury* v. *Madison* emphasizes the facts of the case and the establishment of the principle of judicial review. For example, Bob Jones' high school civics book states, "With this decision John Marshall established the principle of judicial review. According to this doctrine the Supreme Court reserves the right to decide whether a law violates the Constitution. . . . *Marbury* v. *Madison* marks an important step in the development of American constitutional law and was the first significant exercise of the Supreme Court's most powerful check of [sic] legislative and executive actions."[14] A Beka's civics text states that "Marshall gave the Court the right of having the final say in constitutional matters [and] judicial review gave the Supreme Court its most effective tool in checking and balancing Congress and the President," but other texts by the same publishers offer negative views of *Marbury*.[15] The A Beka high school American history text obliquely criticizes the opinion: "By subtle ingenuity [Chief Justice Marshall] had given the Federalist Supreme Court untold authority as a watchdog over Republican legislation."[16] Perhaps more problematic is Bob Jones' current events textbook linking *Marbury* to "judicial activism." The author clearly conveys his disapproval of "judicial activism": "By a free interpretation of the Constitution, sometimes called judicial activism, judges have seized power from the other two branches of government to make policy, or 'legislate from the bench'."[17] Students are told that "generally conservatives favor judicial restraint . . . [because] otherwise there is no firm foundation for law."[18] Moving on to *Marbury* itself, the text notes that, "[i]ronically, John Marshall, a conservative chief justice . . . laid the foundation for judicial activism."[19] Thomas Jefferson's opposition to the *Marbury* decision is described: "He considered [it] a direct assault on republican government [that] would permit the rise of a 'despotic third branch' of unelected officials who rule for life."[20]

In A Beka's civics book, *McCulloch* v. *Maryland* is described as having "established the doctrine of implied powers" through its interpretation of the necessary and proper clause; however, the authors go on to editorialize that "since the 19th century the 'necessary and proper' clause has been interpreted more and more loosely by both Court and Congress."[21] The corresponding Bob Jones text discusses the Court's reasoning by quoting from the opinion and merely states that *McCulloch* "reaffirmed" the principle of judicial review and "extended it to the statehouses and city halls of America."[22] *Gibbons* v. *Ogden* also is linked to the expansion of the powers of the federal government.[23]

The treatment of *Trustees of Dartmouth College* v. *Woodward*[24] more clearly illustrates the tendency to make inferences not clearly supported by the decision itself in order to support a conservative viewpoint. In *Dartmouth College* the Supreme Court held that New Hampshire could not make Dartmouth into a public institution, but A Beka's high school textbook states: "Marshall maintained that [Dartmouth's] charter was a binding contract with which the state could not tamper. Thus, the Supreme Court ruled that a state does not have the right to interfere with the policies of a private college."[25] But, of course, a state does have the right, just as it would with other businesses, to intervene or regulate a private college or university when its policies conflict with the state's constitution or statutes.

Dred Scott v. *Sandford* and *Plessy* v. *Ferguson* are mentioned or discussed 10 times in 10 books or booklets. In marked contrast to the abortion and Establishment Clause cases discussed later in this chapter, none of the textbooks criticizes these decisions; and in only one instance is there even the slightest hint that the cases might have been wrongly decided. A Beka's high school civics text mentions *Dred Scott* only in connection with one of its discussions of abortion: "The Burger Court held that an unborn child was not a living person but rather the 'property' of the mother (much like slaves were consider the property of their masters in the 1857 case of *Dred Scott* v. *Sandford*)."[26] Moreover:

> Chief Justice Taney found that under the Constitution (1) a slave was not a citizen and could not sue in the courts [and] (2) a slave was the property of his owner and that Congress had no power to deprive a citizen of his property. Thus Taney declared the Missouri Compromise to be unconstitutional, which meant a slave owner could now take his slaves to any part of the United States.[27]

This ends the discussion of the *Dred Scott* decision in this particular textbook.

Bob Jones' civics text notes that "the *Dred Scott* decision overturned the Missouri Compromise and helped set the stage for the bloody confrontation between the North and South."[28] The nearest any of these textbooks comes to criticizing the opinion of the Court is to concede that Taney's views were "the most extreme" of the justices when the Chief Justice stated that "the Constitution did not recognize slaves or free blacks as citizens. Blacks, in Taney's words, 'had no rights which the white man was bound to respect'."[29] *Plessy* v. *Ferguson* is treated in similar fashion, primarily as being overturned by *Brown*. For example, a School of Tomorrow/Accelerated Christian Education civics booklet observes that "the separate but equal doctrine laid down in the 1896 case of *Plessy* vs. *Ferguson* was [found] unconstitutional" by the *Brown* decision.[30] Speaking directly of *Plessy* itself, the A Beka high school text states that:

> since 1896 race relations in public schools had been governed by the Supreme Court decision in *Plessy* vs. *Ferguson*. In that landmark decision the Supreme Court had argued on a close 5 to 4 vote that racial segregation in public places did not violate the U.S. Constitution if 'separate but equal' facilities were maintained for both blacks and whites.[31]

Bob Jones' civics textbook also gives *Plessy* a neutral and, it can be argued, in the absence of any criticism of *Plessy* or its results, an almost approving treatment:

> The Kansas law [requiring separate schools for white and African-American children] was in keeping with the 1896 Supreme Court ruling in *Plessy* v. *Ferguson*. In the *Plessy* decision the justices upheld segregated facilities since the XIV Amendment providing "equal protection of the laws" for all citizens referred only to legal equality, not social equality.[32]

Both A Beka's and Bob Jones' high school American history textbooks briefly mention *Panama Refining Company* v. *Ryan* and *United States* v. *Butler*. The selection of these cases for inclusion is consistent with the generally unfavorable treatment accorded Franklin Roosevelt and the New Deal.[33]

First Amendment Cases

First Amendment cases fall into two categories: those concerned with religion and those concerned with freedom of speech.

Religion Cases. Twenty-three religion cases are discussed or mentioned in 49 separate instances. The texts are highly critical of the Court's Establishment Clause jurisprudence. On occasion, the critical tone employed by the authors lapses into open disparagement of the decisions of the Court. For example, the *Lemon* test is described as a "contrivance."[34] To the authors of A Beka's civics book, "The *Lemon* test is truly a lemon."[35] In addition, the authors ascribe a number of adverse consequences to the school prayer and Bible reading decisions in *Engel* v. *Vitale* and *School District of Abington Township* v. *Schempp* (often given combined coverage). Overall, *Engel* and *Schempp* are described as having removed prayer from public education. Very rarely do the textbooks qualify such blanket statements by including phrases such as "state-sanctioned." The phrases "teacher-led prayers" or "school-sponsored prayers," which are more accurate portrayals of the reach of these decisions, are not used.[36] Fourth-graders using A Beka's American history text read that "the Supreme Court ruled that prayer and Bible reading were illegal in public schools [when the Court] ignoring our Christian heritage, interpreted the Constitution in a way that its writers would not have agreed with."[37] In a section titled "O'Hair's Campaign Against God," eighth-graders are told that:

> In 1962, the *Supreme Court removed prayer from public schools*, and in 1963, it banned Bible reading from the public schools. These decisions came about largely through the efforts of Madelyn Murray O'Hair, an *atheist* and *Communist* who used her teen-age son, William, to protest daily Bible reading and prayer in the public schools of Baltimore, Maryland. A liberal Supreme Court ruled that even voluntary Bible reading and prayer were unconstitutional because they "discriminated against" non-Christians.[38]

The text goes on to editorialize:

> The Founding Fathers who wrote the Constitution had great respect for both prayer and God's Word. It was because of our Christian heritage that most schools had included prayer and Bible reading in their daily routines for years. The Supreme Court interpreted the Constitution in a way that its writers would not have agreed with.[39]

The section concludes with an account of William Murray's conversion to Christianity and his regret for the part he played in the case.[40]

The high school book handles the school prayer and Bible reading cases in much the same way, albeit with even stronger language. For example, the *Engel* and *Schempp* plaintiffs are described as "a very vocal and militant minority of atheists and humanists" who were challenging "this public expression [school prayer and Bible reading] of America's faith in the God of her fathers."[41] The authors go on to opine that "the decisions rendered by the courts in the these cases removed all prayer and Bible reading, even on a voluntary basis, from public school class-rooms and went a long way toward establishing secular humanism as the national religion."[42]

Finally, William Murray is described as a person who had been "exploited" by his mother so that she could "press her atheistic ideas on the American public" and who had "lived a pitiful, haunted life [until] he repudiated atheism and Marxism and found faith in God."[43] The section on the *Schempp* case (Ms. O'Hair's case, *Murray* v. *Curlett,* was a companion case to *Schempp*) actually includes a quotation (from an apology by Murray) that is longer than the text's discussion of the case itself.[44] Discussing *Engel* and the putative misuse of Jefferson's "wall of separation," Bob Jones' current events textbook editorializes that "judicial activists . . . have actually made government the enemy of religion."[45]

In School of Tomorrow/Accelerated Christian Education booklets, these decisions are attributed to the justices' substituting their "personal values" for the intent of the Founders that no single denomination be established as a national church.[46] Alluding to Jefferson's Danbury letter, the booklet states, "These men discovered a misleading statement ['separation of church and state'] found in neither the Constitution, the First Amendment, or any other official founding document."[47] This is consistent with the view of the Establishment Clause held by many religious-political conservatives that "by our form of government, the Christian religion is the established religion; and all sects and denominations of Christians are placed on the same equal footing."[48] Unlike the A Beka texts, School of Tomorrow/Accelerated Christian Education explicitly points out that these decisions applied only to state-mandated practices; however, the booklet argues that a number of dire consequences have flowed from *Engel* and *Schempp*, including the decision of the Court in *Stone* v. *Graham*:[49]

> As these decisions were applied, however, states, school boards, and courts of appeals interpreted the rulings as directing that prayer, Bible reading, and posting the Commandments were not permitted in schools [*Stone* v. *Graham*] or in any type of public setting. The result in most communities was the elimination of all three from schools and all public meetings.[50]

Although some individuals and groups might see *Engel* and *Schempp* as having had these consequences, there is simply no evidence that this sweeping generalization is, in fact, true. To the contrary, the Supreme Court upheld legislative prayers in *Marsh* v. *Chambers*.[51] By selective quotation, School of Tomorrow/Accelerated Christian Education misrepresents *Vidal* v. *Girard's Executors*, a 19th century case in which the Court held that a testamentary provision prohibiting the employment of clergy at a school for poor children did not violate state law.[52] The booklet quotes from the opinion so that phrases praising the presence of Christianity in education are emphasized while the holding itself is de-emphasized. Another example of a misleading use of quotations occurs when the booklet states, "In 1811 a lower court made the following ruling, which was later cited by the Supreme Court: 'Whatever strikes at the root of Christianity tends manifestly to the dissolution of civil government'."[53] The Court may have cited the ruling of this unnamed case, but the language quoted in the booklet does not appear in any decision.[54] Not surprisingly, the *Church of the Holy Trinity* v. *United States* dictum is included: "The Supreme Court, after describing at length America's religious history, stated: 'These and many other matters which might be noticed add a volume of unofficial declarations to the mass of organic utterances that this is a Christian nation'."[55] The text goes on, "In making this decision the Court cited numerous historical and judicial precedents," thus eliding the use of precedents with dictum.[56] The phrasing and visual treatment (it is in large, purple, italic type) implies that the quotation is the holding of the case, but it is not. It is a footnote.

By contrast, discussions of free exercise issues are, for the most part, more nuanced. The section devoted to Free Exercise Clause issues in Bob Jones' civics textbook opens with a discussion of *Reynolds* v. *United States*,[57] the 1879 case in which the Court held that polygamy was not protected by the Free Exercise Clause, and includes a relatively lengthy quotation. *Minersville School District* v. *Gobitis* and *West Virginia Board of Education* v. *Barnette*[58] illustrate the "inherent tensions that may arise over an unrestricted interpretation of the free exercise of religion."[59]

The texts exhibit a degree of ambivalence about the Free Exercise Clause that is in distinct contrast to their approach to the Establishment Clause. This ambivalence is two-fold. First, the Free Exercise Clause raises issues related to compliance to generally applicable laws, which is problematic given the texts' emphasis on obedience generally. Second, the texts take a somewhat equivocal and occasionally derogatory stance toward the extension of Free Exercise rights to the religious practices of non-traditional religions, including unconventional expressions of Christianity.

The authors, in a somewhat didactic fashion, stress obedience to the law; and the importance of being a law-abiding citizen is strongly linked to religion: "For the Christian, rendering obedience to the state is not an option, but a commandment."[60] A long scriptural quotation from 1 Peter follows this statement.[61] Keesee opines that "Christians are to obey their government because it is a 'minister of God' in this world. The authority principle is established by God."[62] But ultimately believers must bow to the authority of God over that of the state if a conflict exists: "If the government attempts to force a Christian to do something that violates a clear Biblical commandment and the believer has exhausted every avenue of appeal, then he must obey the higher authority — which is God."[63]

A Beka's civics book resolves this free exercise conundrum by telling its readers that "the right to 'free exercise of religion,' however, is limited in scope; common standards of decency, law, and order may not be violated under the guise of 'freedom of religion'."[64] Of course, the difficulty for conservative Protestants and the writers of these textbooks lies in defining "common standards of decency, law, and order." At times it seems as if, from their perspective, religiously motivated conduct that closely resembles conservative Protestantism meets "common standards of decency, law, and order," while the conduct of faith groups that are less traditional or less favored from an orthodox Protestant perspective does not. Thus the A Beka text goes on to frame its inherent difficulty in approaching the Free Exercise Clause by stating:

> The Court has ruled against snake handling [*McDaniel* v. *Paty*] and the use of illegal drugs by those who claim such practices to be an exercise of their religion [*Employment Division* v. *Smith*]. However, the Court will often uphold unusual religious practices. The Court has ruled, for example, that certain groups have the right to salute the flag (or not salute) the flag [*Gobitis* and *Barnette*], to sacrifice animals [*Church of the Lukumi Babalu Aye* v. *Hialeah*], or to abstain from work on Sunday because of religious convictions [*Sherbert* v. *Verner*].[65]

What is interesting is the authors' focus on the nature of the religious practices, rather than on the issue of the degree of government interest in prohibiting the conduct. This approach also is taken by the Bob Jones' civics text. In the teacher's notes that accompany the section on the courts and the First Amendment, the authors suggest that the teacher "might want to discuss the limits of government interference in such controversial modern cases as snake handlers [*McDaniel*], Indians who use peyote (a banned drug) [*Smith*], faddish cults that use marijuana, and Christian Scientists who withhold medical treatment from their children."[66] Overall, the coverage of Free Exercise Clause cases is less extensive, less internally consistent, less polemic, and more sporadic than that given to Establishment Clause cases.

Freedom of Speech Cases. Like the Free Exercises cases, other First Amendment cases are discussed in the civics books and are either absent or relatively rare in the history texts. The civics books discuss a total of 16 freedom of speech cases. Only two free speech cases, *Roth* v. *United States* and *Schenck* v. *United States*[67] could be found in the U.S. history textbooks. In the A Beka books, more coverage is given to issues related to obscenity and pornography than to "pure" free speech cases, such as *Chaplinsky* v. *New Hampshire* and *Dennis* v. *United States*.[68] By contrast, the Bob Jones text gives considerably more coverage to the development of the Supreme Court's free speech jurisprudence generally. Like its approach to Free Exercise jurisprudence, the Bob Jones text includes a somewhat balanced analysis of the issues involved. For example, "A citizen must be free to criticize the government in general or one of its officials in particular without fear of having his voice silenced by jail walls. On the other hand, the government has a legitimate role in protecting public order."[69] However, the author does appear to be slightly biased in favor of public order and to support the suppression of seditious speech: "The government has a clear right to defend itself against sedition — attempts to undermine its authority and existence."[70] Prosecution of individuals under various sedition statutes is either omitted (although *Dennis* is discussed specifically) or supported. The A Beka text focuses on disruptive speech and shows mild support for the right of the government to restrict disruptive speech by briefly discussing the holdings in *Chaplinsky* and *Dennis*. The text closes its consideration of the topic by addressing the issue of flag burning, that is, *Texas* v. *Johnson*.[71] The authors criticize the decision because, in their opinion, the protection for symbolic speech is not "guaranteed in the Constitution."[72] They find that "the Court has generally ruled [in recent years] in favor of those who 'express themselves with immoral and contemptible behavior'."[73]

Both textbooks condemn recent Supreme Court decisions upholding free speech when the issue is speech that the authors consider immoral: "These decisions [*Cohen* v. *California*, *Rosenfield* v. *New Jersey*, and *Papish* v. *Board of Curators*[74] are specifically named] have paved the way for the further degradation of speech in public discourse."[75] Even decisions in which the Court has upheld the restrictions on speech are faulted because the Court is a national, rather than a local, forum for making such determinations: "The national government is simply not as capable of regulating obscenity as are local communities where the family and church are more prominent and have more influence on community standards."[76] And again, "to move the debate about pornography (obscene writings or pictures designed to arouse immoral thoughts, feelings, and desires) and other obscenities from the local to the national level is to remove it from the area that can best deal with them."[77] Setting aside the partial eliding of pornography with obscenity and the apparent disregard of the provision for the application of local standards set out in *Miller* v. *California*,[78] these passages are entirely consistent with the preference for states' rights and local control that is a recurring theme in these materials. Moreover, because freedom of speech issues arise under the First Amendment, these passages support the sometimes-argued conservative position that the Bill of Rights should not apply to state governments.

As with the Establishment Clause cases discussed previously and the abortion cases discussed below, the Bob Jones text's discussion of obscenity and pornography litigation, though scant, is focused on the social ills engendered by the Court's decisions and the failure of police to adequately enforce existing laws:

> The easing of restraint through weak laws and sometimes weak enforcement has permitted man more freedom, or more correctly, greater bondage in sin. The results have been a proliferation of the pornography industry and increased moral corruption in lives, homes, and communities. The necessity of restricting obscene, violent, and seditious speech is an obvious result of man's sinfulness.[79]

The textbooks also touch briefly on the issue of freedom of assembly, primarily in the A Beka civics book. After noting the legitimacy of "time, place, and manner" restrictions, the authors state that "laws regulating assembly . . . cannot be targeted toward any particular group [and that] when Forsyth County, Georgia officials sought to charge a fee to a white supremacist group for protesting, the Court sided with the protesters."[80] However, almost one-third of the section that treats freedom of assembly jurisprudence is a fairly sharply worded polemic against the anti-war protesters of the 1960s: "These activities on the nation's streets and college campuses often included language of the vilest and most offensive variety."[81] The convictions of the protesters (described as "young anarchists") "were overturned by higher courts on *technicalities*, [but] the Founding Fathers would have stood aghast that such words and deeds could be excused" (emphasis added).[82] The Bob Jones text ties restrictions on freedom of assembly to "man's tendency to abuse his freedom."[83] This view of the inherent depravity of human beings is a fairly common theme throughout the textbooks, especially in their discussions of the rule of law and the relationship of citizens and government.

Abortion Cases

All eight A Beka and Bob Jones textbooks contained references to *Roe* v. *Wade*[84] and all references are critical of the Court's decision. In addition, one Accelerated Christian Education booklet briefly mentions *Roe*. In this section, I take up each publishers' materials separately.

A Beka Books. In a section discussing John Kennedy's presidency, fourth-graders using A Beka textbooks are told, "The 1960s and 1970s saw many liberal court decisions, including *Roe v. Wade* (1973), which legalized abortion, the killing of unborn babies."[85] Grussendorf, Lowman, and Ashbaugh preface the eighth-grade American history text's discussion of *Roe* with the term *liberal*.[86] "The Supreme Court ruled in favor of abortion, the killing of babies before birth."[87] Likewise, in the 11th-grade American history text, the discussion of *Roe* occurs in a section titled "A liberal Supreme Court."[88] The authors describe the Court as ruling in favor of "legalized abortion," which has resulted in "at least 15 million babies [being] murdered" between 1973 and 1983.[89] A Beka's American government text attacks the reasoning underlying the decision itself, as well as the results of the Court's decision:

> Ignoring 3,500 years of Judeo-Christian civilization, religion, morality, and law, the Burger Court held that an unborn child was not a living person but rather "property" of the mother (much like slaves were consider the property of their masters in the 1857 case of *Dred Scott* v. *Sandford*). Hence the Court ruled that the unborn are not entitled to the right of life under the 5th and 14th Amendments. The error of such thinking was obvious. The right of any mother to have the power of life and death over a child is much more than a "right to privacy"; it is a usurpation of God's role in the lives of others, a right that does not reside in the four corners of the Constitution.
>
> The 1973 *Roe* decision was, and continues to be, a devastating one. As a result of *Roe* v. *Wade,* more than 30 million unborn children were killed in abortion mills in the United States alone between 1973 and 1996. More lives have been snuffed out by abortion in America than by all the wars our nation has ever fought.[90]

The text returns to the illegitimacy of a constitutional right to privacy in a discussion of the Ninth Amendment: "Some legal scholars want to use the Ninth Amendment to claim a 'right to privacy' in order to sanction the immorality propagated by abortionists, homosexuals, and any other group that wants to practice moral deviancy with legal protection."[91] The authors go on to argue that "homosexuality and abortion" are without constitutional protection like other conduct that is not specifically addressed in the Constitution. Somewhat pejoratively within the next few lines, the authors cite murder and rape as other examples of conduct unmentioned in the Constitution that prove this point: "Murder and rape are not mentioned in the Constitution either, yet we know that they [like homosexuality and abortion] merit no constitutional protection."[92]

Bob Jones University Press. Eighth-graders using Bob Jones's textbooks are introduced to *Roe* in a short section on the Supreme Court. *Roe* is given a subsection of its own in this discussion. Like the A Beka texts, this discussion starts by characterizing the decision as "liberal."

> Unfortunately the conservatives on the court did not have enough power to prevent a liberal decision on abortion. In *Roe* v. *Wade* (1973), the court decided that a woman had the right to abort her unborn child within the first three months of pregnancy. Since then about 1.5 million abortions have been performed each year. This legalized murder destroys nearly one-third of all American babies each year.[93]

Bob Jones's high school text positions *Roe* in a section that discusses "radical" and "extreme" feminists: "In the landmark case *Roe* v. *Wade* (1973), however, the Supreme Court struck down most state abortion laws. As a result of the Court's decision, the slaughter of unborn children by abortion rose to over one million a year by 1978. Women's liberationists were elated with the decision."[94] Like the A Beka books, the strongest language critical of *Roe* appears in Bob Jones's senior high school civics book, and it is the civics book that attacks the legal underpinnings of the decision:

The most shocking example of the Court's social activism was the 1973 decision *Roe* v. *Wade,* which legalized abortion. The *Roe* decision did not start the practice; abortions by the hundreds of thousands were taking place in America before 1973. Rather it placed the stamp of judicial approval upon it and in so doing encouraged and increased the procedure. With 1.6 million abortions performed annually, the grisly operation has become as common as a tonsillectomy, only cheaper. The courts have extended the XIV Amendment right to "life, liberty, and property" to every conceivable group — except the unborn.[95]

Keesee is as critical of the Court's reasoning as he is of the consequences: "The controversy over the *Roe* v. *Wade* decision centers on the Supreme Court's unwarranted extension of constitutional protections at the expense of precedent, state jurisdiction, scientific evidence, and sound moral reason."[96] The teacher's notes that accompany this portion of the text state that "*Roe* v. *Wade* is a shocking example of how Supreme Court activism can support a gross evil in society as abortion."[97] Keesee goes on to describe *Planned Parenthood* v. *Ashcroft,*[98] as an "example of chronic irrationality on the subject [of abortion]."[99] More general pro-life material appears in this section than in any of the other Bob Jones textbooks or the A Beka books, including the statement that "abortion clinics . . . embody the nation's moral decline [and are] a monument to man's failed attempt to achieve the goal of justice."[100] A full-page highlighted text box titled "Abortion Atrocities" describes in some detail the techniques of curettage, suction curettage, and saline and chemically induced abortions:[101] "Sharp curettage involves a knife killing the fetus . . . in suction curettage, a vacuum pump sucks out the fetus in bits (a knife cleans out any remnants)."[102] "[In saline-induced abortions] the salt seems to act as a poison; the skin of the fetus, when delivered, resembles skin soaked in acid."[103] "The fetus can be in this solution for two hours before its heart (a stubborn bit of 'potential life') stops beating."[104] The text goes on to discuss the issue of fetal pain: "We infer, and empathize with, the pain of creatures,

such as baby seals, which lack language to express pain. . . ."
(ellipsis in the original).[105] This material also alludes to *Planned
Parenthood of Missouri* v. *Danforth*.[106] "Planned Parenthood, the
most extreme pro-abortion lobby, won a Supreme Court ruling
that it is unconstitutional to ban the saline abortion technique.
That's right. The court discovered that the 'privacy' right to abortion, which right the framers of the Constitution neglected to mention, even confers a right to a particular abortion technique."[107]

School of Tomorrow/Accelerated Christian Education. Although material on abortion generally appears in both U.S. history and American government booklets, discussion of *Roe* itself
(in a second government text) is relatively short and, in contrast
to the A Beka and Bob Jones civics textbooks, mild: "Even more
shocking than [the Establishment Clause decisions] was the 1973
Roe v. *Wade* decision which legalized abortion. Since that date,
millions of innocent babies have been killed with the approval of
the Supreme Court."[108]

School Desegregation Cases

Only two school desegregation cases, *Brown* and *Swann* (the
latter is not mentioned by name), are included in the texts, though
Bob Jones's eighth-grade history text alludes to the higher education cases that preceded *Brown*. Like *Roe*, *Brown* is discussed
or mentioned in every textbook and in one School of Tomor-
row/Accelerated Christian Education booklet; however, the coverage of *Brown* is split between sections dealing with civil rights
(primarily in the history textbooks) and discussions of the legal
system in the civics texts. For the most part, the treatment is neutral and the absence of indignation or passionate language, common in discussions of abortion or Establishment Clause issues, is
noticeable. For example, A Beka's civics book exemplifies both
the placement in context (federal power versus states' rights) and
the dry, factual approach to the legal issues related to race and
civil rights:

In the past, it was not unusual for the Supreme Court to declare a state law unconstitutional, but the Court rarely told the states what they must do. All of this changed after 1955 with the *Brown* v. *Board of Education II* court case, when Courts began compelling states to desegregate their public schools. (Previously, black students and white students had attended separate schools.)[109]

Bob Jones's current events text criticizes the decision as an example of judicial activism, noting that no legal precedents were cited:

While the end was a noble one — ending discrimination in schools — the means were troublesome. The equal protection of the law clause of the Fourteenth Amendment protected an individual's equal right to a fair trial [echoing the Court's reasoning in *Plessy*]. But the *Brown* decision questioned not only legal equality but also social equality.[110]

The text goes on to opine that "liberals were not willing to wait for a political solution."[111]

The authors of two A Beka history texts mention opposition to busing without the Court's reasons supporting this remedy or any positive results that flowed from its use to desegregate public schools: "One very controversial way to end segregation in the schools involved court-ordered busing of students from one school district to another."[112] The same language appears in the publisher's high school textbook and, as with *Brown* itself, the busing decisions of the Court are linked to the issue of federalism: "Parents of all races and ethnic groups were upset that their children no longer attended neighborhood schools. Local school districts became increasingly dependent on money grants controlled by administrative agencies based in Washington, D.C. Any objections to federal policies were often overruled by the need for federal funds."[113]

Miscellaneous Cases

As previously stated, these cases include those related to criminal law (five cases) and other issues, including federalism, voting rights, civil litigation brought against a sitting president, birth control, gun-free school zones, and firearms. Unlike the historical cases, no clear pattern of coverage emerges. The A Beka civics textbook discusses six of these 12 cases, while the Bob Jones civics text discusses seven. These discussions are scattered throughout the history books from both A Beka and Bob Jones University Press.

The A Beka texts focus on death penalty cases, while Bob Jones' books also include other criminal law issues (Miranda warnings, right to assistance of counsel, exclusion of illegally obtained evidence). The A Beka civics book merely gives the holdings of *Furman* v. *Georgia* and *Gregg* v. *Georgia*,[114] though not the bases on which the Court reached its decisions. It asserts that the Eighth Amendment does not prohibit the death penalty and ties the Eighth Amendment to scripture: "This amendment follows the Biblical principle that the penalty or the punishment for a crime should match the severity of the crime."[115] By contrast, the publisher's U.S. history books ascribe the rise in crime subsequent to 1972 to the Supreme Court's decision in *Furman* and tying the decision to "several liberal decisions . . . indicating the moral decline of the nation as a whole."[116] The publisher's high school texts use the same language.

The Bob Jones civics book is more factual in its approach to the death penalty cases, noting that the Court found that "all state death penalty statutes were too vague and too inconsistently applied."[117] However, a highlighted text box on the facing page instructs students in "What . . . the Bible Say[s] About Capital Punishment."[118] This material quotes scripture ("Whosoever sheddest a man's blood, by man shall his blood be shed.") and opines, "Scripture is clear that God still expects government exercise appropriate use of the death penalty"[119] and that "the sword . . . is an instrument of punishment which God requires the state to wield for the cause of justice; and for bloody men who take life, the death penalty is just."[120]

Bob Jones' texts also address major criminal procedures cases, *Gideon* v. *Wainwright*, *Miranda* v. *Arizona*, and *Mapp* v. *Ohio*.[121]

In the high school American history text, *Gideon* is presented in fairly straightforward fashion; but the authors include the following statements at the end of the material dealing with *Miranda*:

> Rigid requirements [such] as the Miranda rule have sometimes prevented police from keeping criminals off the street, when technical violations of their rights occurred. Crimes from murder to drunk driving have been dismissed in the face of overwhelming evidence because of rights violation. Such incidents reveal a warped sense of priority on the part of the courts — when rights are placed above justice.[122]

Overall, the texts are strongly supportive of states' rights. The A Beka civics text describes federal intrusions into matters the authors consider the proper prerogative of the states as "coercive federalism."[123] The Supreme Court is described as "having coerced the states into submission" through the incorporation of the due process clause of the Fourteenth Amendment.[124] The discussion of *Garcia* v. *San Antonio Metropolitan Authority* is placed in a section titled "Gutting the 10th Amendment."[125]

The discussion of the apportionment cases also emphasizes the issue of state autonomy and portrays these decisions as wrongly decided and having negative results. The holding in *Reynolds* v. *Sims*[126] is criticized because "the Court insisted upon [the] argument [based on the equal protection clause of the Fourteenth Amendment] in spite of the fact that the same Constitution which guarantees equal protection under the law also establishes a Congress of the United States with one house (the Senate) based solely upon geographical boundaries (state boundaries) without regard for population."[127] The results of the case are described as having "intimidated . . . the states."[128] Because of this intimidation, "the states fell into line."[129]

The Bob Jones history text takes a similar, albeit more subtle, view of the apportionment cases. *Reynolds* is not named but is described as a "typical case of judicial activism."[130] After quoting Justice Harlan's dissent, the authors editorialize that "unfortunately, the majority of Harlan's associates did not listen to him."[131] The authors of the A Beka text see "a glimmer of hope" with the Court's overturning of the Gun Free School Zone Act in *United States* v. *Lopez*.[132] By its decision, the Court "banned Congress from policing local school zones."[133] The authors do not discuss the subject of the act itself, that is, that the act would have banned the carrying of handguns within a certain distance of schools.

As in their handling of politics and government generally, the authors of these textbooks express extremely conservative views of the Supreme Court's constitutional jurisprudence, though perhaps less noticeably so than in their approach to the broader subjects of government and politics. Here, their conservative point of view manifests itself less by what is said than by how it is presented. For example, disparities in the amount of coverage between abortion and civil rights — and the nature of the discussion, including explicit and implicit criticism of certain decisions — make clear the position of the authors on a number of topics. The texts show a marked preference for 1) a more restricted role for the judiciary, except for activism in areas consistent with conservative positions; 2) states' rights; and 3) originalism in constitutional interpretation.

Concluding Comments

A preference for strict constitutional construction is hardly surprising, given the authors' insistence on a literal interpretation of the Bible. Moreover, returning to Lakoff's analysis, introduced at the end of Chapter Two, it is clear that when morality depends on clear authority, subjectivity poses a real risk to the proper order of society. Thus judicial review based on *Marbury* poses a danger to the hierarchical structure.

In the same manner, these authors' attitudes toward criminal law reflect an adherence to both Lakoff's Moral Order and Moral Authority metaphors.[134] The Moral Order metaphor sets out hierarchical relationships based on "moral authority and dominance: God over human beings, men over women, adults over children, etc."[135] According to this view, restrictions on police powers, such as the *Miranda* rule, impede the ability of the police to maintain the proper order. These authors' strong support for the death penalty epitomizes the retributive aspect of Lakoff's Moral Accounting.[136] Similarly, the emphasis in the Free Speech cases is on the danger of unrestricted speech. The texts pay lip service to the idea of free speech, especially in the area of political speech; but their authors explicitly point out the dangers of pornography, which may lead to immorality, and seditious speech, which would be immoral because it challenges the moral order.

As we have seen in both the previous chapter and this one, much attention and extremely strong rhetoric is focused on the issue of abortion. Lakoff notes, and the authors of these textbooks exemplify, how conservatives frame discussions of abortion in terms of "baby killing," while liberals espouse their position by evoking a medical model and using such medical terminology as "fetus" and "embryo."[137] In these textbooks, the terms "fetus" and "embryo" are almost never used. The language is that of murder, and the analogies are to the Holocaust and slavery in the American South. Abortion itself is a profound challenge to the moral order and the moral authority that supports it. Hence it assumes great prominence in these materials, and the authors suppress dissenting views.

Overall, the authors favor responsibilities over rights, and this preference underlies their handling of civil rights cases. This is exemplified by their failure to condemn the *Dred Scott* and *Plessy* decisions, coupled with their lukewarm and occasionally critical coverage of *Brown*.

Conservatives see the school prayer decisions as attacks on the proper moral order. The textbooks present as unmitigated evils those Establishment Clause cases that restrict their rights to express their religious views, or at least religious expression to which they can subscribe. This is why *Engel* and *Schempp* are so harshly condemned. Defense of moral order is virtuous; by attacking the Court directly on this issue, the authors are themselves acting morally.

It is clear that the authors of these textbooks intend to inculcate a set of strongly conservative beliefs. The question then becomes whether it is proper for the government to subsidize schools whose curricula are so highly imbued with partisan political material. There is little, if any, distinction between using taxpayer funds, directly or indirectly, to support advocacy organizations of whatever persuasion and schools that use the curricula described in these two chapters.

In Chapters Four and Five I will describe the religious bias that is pervasive throughout these textbooks by focusing on their attitudes toward Roman Catholicism and non-Western religions.

Notes

1. The title of this chapter appeared in a political cartoon by Don Addis in the *St. Petersburg Times* and was sent to me by a colleague. This chapter is based on an earlier article, published in the *Journal of Law & Education* 29 (August 2000): 405-31.
2. Although this article focuses on these 18 booklets, quotations from one elementary and two junior high school social studies booklets also have been included where relevant.
3. See Timothy Keesee, *American Government for Christian Schools, Teacher's Edition* (Greenville, S.C.: Bob Jones University Press, 1998), p. 83.
4. Historical cases include cases decided before 1950, especially where they are no longer good law; some cases could arguably be considered civil rights cases, though in a negative sense. See, for example, *Dred Scott v. Sandford*, 60 U.S. (19 How.) 393 (1857); *Plessy v. Ferguson*, 163 U.S. 537 (1896). However, in some instances, pre-1950 cases were included as specific types of cases, such as religion or freedom of speech cases. See, for example, *Minersville School Dist. v. Gobitis*, 310 U.S. 586 (1940); *Chaplinsky v. New Hampshire*, 315 U.S. 568 (1942) (advocating freedom of speech).
5. *Jones v. Clinton*, 520 U.S. 945 (1997).
6. *Griswold v. Connecticut*, 381 U.S. 479 (1965).
7. *Brown v. Board of Education*, 347 U.S. 483 (1954).
8. *Roe v. Wade*, 410 U.S. 113 (1973). Abortion as a general issue is discussed 20 times, and it is discussed in all eight textbooks and two ACE booklets. Included are discussions of *Roe v. Wade*,

Planned Parenthood of Southeastern Pennsylvania v. *Casey*, and *Webster* v. *Reproductive Health Services*. In addition, there are two cases the texts do not name, *Planned Parenthood of Missouri* v. *Danforth* and *Planned Parenthood of Kansas City* v. *Ashcroft*, which discuss or mention abortion 32 times. Some of this material is quite lengthy, highly detailed, and in some instances technical.

9. *Marbury* v. *Madison*, 5 U.S. (1 Cranch) 137 (1803).
10. *Engel* v. *Vitale*, 370 U.S. 421 (1962).
11. *Plessy* v. *Ferguson*, 163 U.S. 537 (1896).
12. *Abington School Dist.* v. *Schempp*, 374 U.S. 203 (1963).
13. *Marbury* v. *Madison*, 5 U.S. 137 (1803); *McCulloch* v. *Maryland*, 17 U.S. 316 (1819); *Trustees of Dartmouth College* v. *Woodward*, 17 U.S. (4 Wheat.) 518 (1819); *Gibbons* v. *Ogden*, 22 U.S. 1 (1824); *Dred Scott* v. *Sandford*, 60 U.S. 393 (1856); *Plessy* v. *Ferguson*, 163 U.S. 537 (1896); *Panama Refining Co.* v. *Ryan*, 292 U.S. 388 (1935); *United States* v. *Butler*, 297 U.S. 1 (1936); and *Northern Sec. Comp.* v. *United States*, 193 U.S. 197 (1904).
14. Keesee, op. cit., p. 289.
15. William R. Bowen et al., *American Government in Christian Perspective*, 2nd ed. (Pensacola, Fla.: A Beka, 1997), p. 147.
16. Michael R. Lowman, George Thompson, and Kurt Grussendorf, *United States History in Christian Perspective: Heritage of Freedom*, 2nd ed. (Pensacola, Fla.: A Beka, 1996), p. 163.
17. *Teacher's Resource Guide to Current Events for Christian Schools, 1998-1999* (Greenville, S.C.: Bob Jones University Press, 1998), p. 33.
18. Ibid.
19. Ibid.
20. Ibid. An interesting view of the intent of the Founders regarding the role of Supreme Court justices is expressed in an eighth-grade School of Tomorrow/Accelerated Christian Education booklet: "The founding fathers thought of the justices as prophets of God who would speak out whenever the government or the people violated God's law." *Social Studies 1088*, rev. 1998 (n.p.: Accelerated Christian Education, 1990), p. 23 . See also Chapter Two for a discussion of theocracy.
21. Bowen et al., op. cit., p. 183.

22. Keesee, op. cit., p. 290.

23. Ibid.

24. 17 U.S. (4 Wheat.) 518 (1819).

25. Lowman, Thompson, and Grussendorf, op. cit., p. 183.

26. Bowen et al., op. cit., p. 151.

27. Kurt A. Grussendorf, Michael R. Lowman, and Brian S. Ashbaugh, *America: Land That I Love, Teacher's Edition.* (Pensacola, Fla.: A Beka, 1994), p. 279.

28. Keesee, op. cit., p. 289. Keesee does not give the facts of the case, but notes that it revived the principle of judicial review.

29. See Timothy Keesee and Mark Sidwell, *United States History for Christian Schools* (Pensacola, Fla.: A Beka, 1991), p. 273.

30. See *Social Studies, U.S. Civics-4 (#1136)* (n.p.: Accelerated Christian Education, 1997), p. 20.

31. Lowman, Thompson, and Grussendorf, op. cit., p. 607.

32. Keesee, op. cit., p. 291. The holding of the Court is stated as true inasmuch as Keesee does not insert a phrase such as "since the justice found that. . . ."

33. In *Panama Refining Co.* v. *Ryan*, the Court decided that the National Recovery Act was unconstitutional. *United States* v. *Butler* decided that the Agricultural Adjustment Act was unconstitutional. See Chapter Two for a discussion of the disparities in the treatment of Democratic and Republican presidents.

34. See Bowen et al., op. cit., p. 158. Under the *Lemon* test, a law or government policy or practice violates the Establishment Clause if it lacks a secular or nonreligious purpose, advances or inhibits religion, or excessively entangles government with religion. *Lemon* v. *Kurtzman*, 403 U.S. 756 (1971).

35. Ibid.

36. This lack of precision is not unique to Christian school textbooks. A chart in Houghton Mifflin's high school civics book (written for use in public schools, though it can be used in sectarian schools as well) states the Court's holding in *Engel* as "prayer in public schools is unconstitutional" and gives the holding of *Schempp* as "Bible reading in public schools violates the establishment clause." See Richard J. Hardy, *Government in America* (Boston: Houghton Mifflin, 1993), pp. 508-10.

37. *The History of Our United States, Teacher Edition* (Pensacola, Fla.: A Beka, 1998), p. 299. Students also are told that the subse-

quent decline of the public schools led to an increase in Christian school enrollment. The desire to escape desegregation as a cause of this increase is not mentioned.

38. Grussendorf, Lowman, and Ashbaugh, op. cit., p. 470 (instructional emphasis omitted). The focus on the *Murray* plaintiffs, rather than *Schempp* (*Murray* was a companion case) itself or the legal reasoning of the Court, is interesting. By framing the discussion in this manner, the authors can attack the motivation of the plaintiffs and also imply that the decision discriminates against religious people. This theme of discrimination is pervasive throughout religious-conservative literature and commentary, which also, not unexpectedly, includes strong condemnations of atheists and atheism.

39. Ibid. Note that the final phrase, "interpreted the Constitution . . . agreed with" is identical to the previously quoted language in the publisher's fourth-grade text. Although the purpose of this article is to examine Christian school textbooks, rather than to compare these sectarian textbooks with those that are used in public schools, the occasional inclusion of material from a secular publisher is instructive. The secular Houghton Mifflin text discusses *Engel* in the following paragraphs:

> One very emotional church-state issue is the question of prayer in the public schools. For years, children in many public schools throughout the United States began each day with a prayer. In New York state, the Board of Regents wrote a prayer for school use: "Almighty God, we acknowledge our dependence upon Thee, and beg Thy blessings upon us, our parents, our teachers, and our country."
>
> The parents of ten public school children in New Hyde Park, N.Y., objected to the Regents' prayer and began the first case on this issue. In *Engel* v. *Vitale* (1962) the parents argued that the prayer violated the establishment clause. A majority of the Supreme Court agreed. Justice Black delivered the majority opinion:
>
> We think that by using its public school system to encourage recitation of the Regents' prayer, the state of New York has adopted a practice wholly inconsistent with the establishment clause. . . .We think that in this country it is no part of the business of government to compose

official prayers for any group of the American people to recite. (Hardy, op. cit., p. 146 [quoting *Engel* v. *Vitale*, 370 U.S. 421, 424-25 (1962)]; Grussendorf, Lowman, and Ashbaugh, op. cit., p. 470)

40. Grussendorf, Lowman, and Ashbaugh, op. cit., p. 470.

41. Lowman, Thompson, and Grussendorf, op. cit., p. 622.

42. Ibid.

43. Ibid.

44. Ibid. Murray apologizes for his lack of faith and how this has damaged the nation. Interestingly, he refers to his mother by her first and last name. "Being raised an atheist in the home of Madelyn O'Hair" (p. 622). Another anomaly of this section is the misspelling of the defendant's name as Carlett.

45. *Teacher's Resource Guide to Current Events*, p. 34.

46. See *Social Studies, U.S. Civics-4* (#1136), p. 29; *Social Studies, U.S. Civics-2* (#1134) (n.p.: Accelerated Christian Education, 1997), p. 31. Fourth-graders are introduced to this somewhat narrow view of the Founders' intent when Mr. Peace, a "Christian lawyer," explains, "The church and state are meant to be separate. That means that the state cannot set up one church as the only church." *Social Studies 1047*, rev. 1998 (n.p.: Accelerated Christian Education, 1981), pp. 17, 21.

47. See *Social Studies, U.S. Civics-2* (#1134), p. 29.

48. Ibid. This quotation, which is highlighted in the text by being in a larger, purple, italic font, is attributed to a 1799 decision by an unnamed "lower court." A drawing of a blue bird is placed beside each highlighted quotation. The text also implies that this was the view of the Founders by placing the following sentence two lines after this quotation: "Obviously today's definition of [the separation of church and state] is far from the beliefs of the founders of our nation" (p. 29).

49. *Stone* v. *Graham*, 449 U.S. 1104 (1981).

50. *Social Studies, U.S. Civics-4* (#1136), p. 30.

51. *Marsh* v. *Chambers*, 463 U.S. 783 (1983). *Marsh* v. *Chambers* is addressed obliquely in A Beka's civics book: "Congress is allowed to hire a chaplain at the taxpayers' expense to open Congress in prayer, yet children are discouraged from praying in public schools (in some places forbidden). Public schools may not have chaplains, but the armed forces may." Bowen et al., op. cit., p. 158.

Note the intermingling of holdings and alleged subsequent applications of the decision.

52. *Vidal* v. *Girard's Executors*, 43 U.S. 127 (1844), p. 199.

53. *Social Studies, U.S. Civics-2* (#1134), p. 29. This quotation is emphasized by being printed in larger, purple, italic type.

54. This language, which paraphrases a 1729 British case, appears in *People* v. *Ruggles*, 8 Johns. 290, 293 (N.Y. 1811) (upholding a jail sentence and fine for blasphemy). In *Roth* v. *United States*, 354 U.S. 476 (1957), the Supreme Court cited, but did not quote, *Ruggles* for the proposition that blasphemy had been a crime under state statute. An action alert of the Christian Coalition of Georgia attributes the quotation to "James Kent, Chief Justice of the Supreme Court of MY [sic] and the Head of the Court of Chancery for nine years" and states that the quotation was included in the August 1999 church bulletin distributed by the organization. Sadie Fields, "Exciting News!! Church Bulletin Insert!!" (Marietta, Ga.: Christian Coalition of Georgia, 1999 [visited Jan. 21, 2000]), available from http://www.cedarproductions.com/gacc/action.htm. In addition to the "root of Christianity" language, the website included additional language from *Ruggles*: "The people of this state, in common with the people of this country, profess the general doctrines of Christianity, as the rule of their faith and practice. . . . We are a Christian people, and the morality of the country is deeply engrafted upon Christianity, and not upon the doctrines or worship of those imposters (other religions)." The phrase "other religions" does not appear in *Ruggles*. The Christian Coalition of Georgia has since moved its website to http://www.gachristian-coalition.org, but the document is not included at the new website.

55. *Social Studies, U.S. Civics-2 (#1134)*, p. 28, quoting *Church of the Holy Trinity* v. *United States*, 143 U.S. 457 (1892).

56. Ibid. The *Holy Trinity* dictum is frequently quoted in conservative religious-political materials. The fact that the statement is dictum is omitted.

57. *Reynolds* v. *United States*, 98 U.S. 145 (1879).

58. *Minersville School Dist.* v. *Gobitis*, 310 U.S. 586 (1943); *West Virginia Board of Educ.* v. *Barnette*, 319 U.S. 624 (1943).

59. Keesee, op. cit., p. 124.

60. Ibid., p. 9.

61. Ibid., citing 1 Pet. 2:13-17.
62. Ibid. In the teacher's notes, Keesee writes, "Men have sinful natures that need to be restricted. When a man breaks a law or threatens the public order, his freedom needs to be restricted" (p. 140). School of Tomorrow/Accelerated Christian Education materials combine fatalism and theology in discussing humanity's penchant for rebelliousness. "God sometimes places harsh governments over people who rebel against him." *Social Studies 1085*, p. 31.
63. Ibid.
64. See Bowen et al., op cit., p. 158. This statement precedes a brief discussion of the *Reynolds* case.
65. Ibid. The cases referred to are: *McDaniel* v. *Paty*, 435 U.S. 618 (1978) (Tennessee statute prohibiting ministers from serving in state legislature violated the Free Exercise Clause). The "ruling" is in a footnote listing several citations to state cases that the Court had declined to hear (p. 627). *Employment Div.* v. *Smith*, 494 U.S. 872 (1990). *Church of the Lukumi Babalu Aye* v. *Hialeah*, 508 U.S. 520 (1993). *Sherbert* v. *Verner*, 374 U.S. 398 (1963).
66. Keesee, op. cit., pp. 140-41.
67. *Roth* v. *United States*, 77 S.Ct. 17 (1956); *Schenck* v. *United States*, 249 U.S. 47 (1919).
68. *Chaplinsky* v. *New Hampshire*, 315 U.S. 568 (1942); *Dennis* v. *United States*, 341 U.S. 494 (1951).
69. Keesee, op. cit., p. 125.
70. Ibid.
71. *Texas* v. *Johnson*, 491 U.S. 397, 406 (1989) (burning the American flag was expressive conduct, that is, symbolic speech, protected by the First Amendment).
72. Bowen et al., op. cit., p. 159.
73. Ibid. The source of the quotation is not given. A Lexis-Nexis search failed to return any Supreme Court decisions using this language. Given the phrasing of the sentence, it is not unreasonable to assume that at least some students would attribute this language, "express[ing] themselves with immoral and contemptible behavior," to a Supreme Court decision.
74. *Cohen* v. *California*, 403 U.S. 15 (1971) (arrest of individual under breach of peace statute for wearing jacket with four-letter expletive violated the First Amendment); *Rosenfield* v. *New*

Jersey, 120 N.J. Super. 458 (N.J. Super. App. Div. 1972) (use of loud and offensive language at public meeting violated state disorderly persons statute), vacated, 408 U.S. 901 (1972); *Papish* v. *Board of Curators*, 410 U.S. 667 (1973) (vulgar cartoon and language in university newspaper was constitutionally protected speech under the First Amendment).

75. Bowen et al., op. cit., p. 159.
76. Ibid.
77. Ibid.
78. 413 U.S. 15 (1973).
79. Keesee, op. cit., p. 127.
80. Bowen et al., op. cit., p. 161.
81. Ibid.
82. Ibid.
83. Keesee, op. cit., p. 127.
84. 410 U.S. 113 (1973).
85. *The History of Our United States*, p. 299. Although "abortion" is not listed in the index, the word is defined in the glossary as the "killing of unborn babies" (p. 320).
86. Grussendorf, Lowman, and Ashbaugh, op. cit., p. 481.
87. Ibid.
88. Lowman, Thompson, and Grussendorf, op. cit., pp. 639-40.
89. Ibid., p. 640.
90. Bowen et al., op. cit., p. 151.
91. Ibid., p. 166.
92. Ibid., p. 167. A secular text treats *Roe* v. *Wade* in a far more neutral fashion:

> A far more controversial ruling [than *Griswold* v. *Connecticut*] based on the Ninth Amendment was made eight years later. In *Roe* v. *Wade* (1973), the Court overturned a Texas law that made abortion illegal. They found the law a violation of the right to privacy under the Ninth and Fourteenth Amendments. Specifically, the Court ruled that in the first three months of pregnancy, women have the right to decide for themselves, without government interference, whether to have an abortion. States were allowed to set limits on abortion in the later months of pregnancy, however.

In the years since *Roe*, the controversy surrounding legal abortion has grown. In 1986 the Supreme Court reaffirmed a woman's right to seek an abortion (*Thornburgh v. American College of Obstetricians and Gynecologists*). Yet in 1991 the Court ruled that federal regulations could prevent workers in federally funded clinics from discussing abortion with their patients (*Rust* v. *Sullivan*). Just two years before, the Court had upheld a Missouri statute in *Webster* v. *Reproductive Health Services* (1989). That law barred public funds from being spent on abortion and ordered doctors to perform fetal-viability tests on women seeking abortions after 20 or more weeks of pregnancy. Since Webster, several other states and territories have passed laws severely limiting the circumstances under which a woman can receive a legal abortion. (Hardy, op. cit., pp. 188-89)

93. *The American Republic for Christian Schools, Teachers Edition* (Greenville, S.C.: Bob Jones University Press, 1988), p. 591.

94. Keesee and Sidwell, op. cit., p. 604.

95. Keesee, op. cit., p. 293.

96. Ibid.

97. Ibid. The student activity to accompany this lesson suggests that the class "Discuss the Scripture verses in the text regarding abortion. Point out how this sin reflects the moral degeneracy and gross selfishness of society" (p. 293).

98. 462 U.S. 476 (1983).

99. Keesee, p. 293. In *Ashcroft*, the Court held that a state may require the presence of a second physician to save a fetus that is delivered alive. *Planned Parenthood* v. *Ashcroft*, p. 494.

100. Ibid. This statement appears directly after a quotation from Proverbs regarding the "hands that shed innocent blood" (p. 293, quoting Prov. 6:17). It is consistent with one of the overarching themes of all of these textbooks, including social studies and English books not addressed in this work, that humanity's efforts to improve its situation are futile (for example, the United Nations) and that only God's intervention will improve the human condition or alleviate suffering.

101. Ibid., p. 292.

102. Ibid., quoting George F. Will, *The Morning After* (New York: Free Press, 1986), pp. 167-68.

103. Ibid.
104. Ibid.
105. Ibid.
106. 428 U.S. 52 (1976). In *Danforth*, the Court held that the state could not require the use of a relatively unavailable method (using prostaglandin) as opposed to the much more common saline amniocentesis method (p. 75).
107. Keesee, op. cit., p. 293.
108. *Social Studies, U.S. Civics-4*, p. 30 (citation omitted).
109. Bowen et al., op. cit., p. 184. This passage constitutes the entire discussion of *Brown* in this textbook.
110. *Teacher's Resource Guide to Current Events*, p. 34. The texts make the same point in connection with slavery and the abolitionists, faulting the abolitionists for their radicalism caused by their unwillingness to wait for a solution to the problem of slavery.
111. Ibid.
112. Grussendorf, Lowman, and Ashbaugh, op. cit., p. 481. This actually is a misleading statement because the Court held in *Milliken v. Bradley*, 418 U.S. 717 (1974), that interdistrict remedies can not be imposed absent evidence of intentional discrimination by an adjacent white majority district (pp. 745, 748, 757). Furthermore, no evidence of widespread interdistrict busing exists to support the authors' contention.
113. Lowman, Thompson, and Grussendorf, op. cit., p. 640.
114. *Furman v. Georgia*, 408 U.S. 238 (1972); *Gregg v. Georgia*, 428 U.S. 153 (1976).
115. Bowen et al., op. cit., p. 166.
116. Grussendorf, Lowman, and Ashbaugh, op. cit., p. 481. This text is designed for eighth-grade students.
117. Keesee, op. cit., p. 132.
118. Ibid., p. 133.
119. Ibid., quoting Gen. 6:9.
120. Ibid., p. 133.
121. *Gideon v. Wainwright*, 372 U.S. 335 (1963); *Miranda v. Arizona*, 384 U.S. 436 (1966); *Mapp v. Ohio*, 367 U.S. 643 (1961).
122. Keesee, op. cit., p. 132.
123. Bowen et al., op. cit., p. 182. "Today there does not seem to be any true limit on the power of Congress, even with the enumer-

ated powers of Article I and the 10th Amendment." Bowen at al., p. 185.

124. Ibid., p. 184.
125. Ibid., p. 185. *Garcia* v. *San Antonio Metropolitan Auth.*, 469 U.S. 528 (1985).
126. 377 U.S. 533 (1964).
127. Bowen et al., op. cit., p. 185.
128. Ibid., p. 185.
129. Ibid., p. 198.
130. Keesee and Sidwell, op. cit., p. 567.
131. Ibid.
132. Bowen et al., op. cit., p. 187.
133. Ibid.
134. George Lakoff, *Moral Politics: What Conservatives Know That Liberals Don't* (Chicago: University of Chicago Press, 1996), pp. 76-84, 104-106.
135. Ibid., p. 105.
136. Ibid., pp. 80-81.
137. Ibid., pp. 263-65, 268.

CHAPTER FOUR

Reformation Redux: Anti-Catholic Bias in Christian School Textooks

To say that the authors of the A Beka and Bob Jones University Press textbooks and School of Tomorrow/Accelerated Christian Education materials portray Roman Catholicism and non-Western religions in a negative way is to understate the case by several orders of magnitude. All the texts evince a deep hostility to these religions. These faiths are continually disparaged and, on rare occasions, ridiculed. Although overt anti-Catholic bias can be found in Bob Jones University Press textbooks, it is most prevalent in books published by A Beka Books.

In this chapter, I describe the denigration of the Roman Catholic Church, its teachings, and its adherents. One particularly striking aspect of the texts is the sense that the battles, or at least the theological battles, of the Protestant Reformation continue unabated to the present day. In the next chapter, I consider how the texts treat various non-Western religions, such as Buddhism, Hinduism, Islam, and the religions of the indigenous peoples of Africa, Asia, Australia, and North America. To do so I draw on a wider range of the textbooks and materials than I used in Chapters Two and Three by including substantially more material from world history and geography textbooks and, in some instances, from the publishers' English literature texts.

Anti-Catholic bias is a part of the American experience and formed a substantial component of nativist movements throughout the country's history. Even anti-Catholicism in American textbooks is not a new phenomenon. Elson discovered that "no theme in [pre-1870] schoolbooks is more universal than anti-Catholicism."[1] Elson gives a number of examples, such as "The Roman Catholic Church completed [the] degeneracy and ruin [of the Holy Roman Empire,"[2] or, more stridently, "the Christian world was distinguished by little more than *name* from pagans and idolators."[3] Many of the techniques that are used in contemporary Christian school textbooks to denigrate Catholicism, which are described in this chapter, also are found in the 19th century textbooks examined by Elson. Among these techniques are the inclusion, often with gratuitous detail, of Catholic persecution of Protestants without counterbalancing coverage of Protestant persecution of Catholics and the omission or negative coverage of Catholic missionaries and their work.[4]

It should be noted from the outset that the anti-Catholicism present in these textbooks, unlike anti-Catholic prejudice in traditional American nativism, does not include any antiforeign elements. Bob Jones' high school English textbook may provide at least a partial explanation of this phenomenon. After discussing the immigration of large numbers of Roman Catholics during the 19th century, the text tells students, "Since Vatican Council II (1962-1964) Roman Catholic leaders have opened dialogue with liberal Protestants in the hopes of undoing the work of the Protestant Reformation."[5] In these textbooks, implicit and explicit bias against Roman Catholics and the Catholic Church is exclusively theological, rather than sociocultural.

Generally, explicit anti-Catholic statements occur most frequently in world history texts and, within those texts, in the sections devoted to early church history, medieval Europe, and, not surprisingly, the Reformation. One exception to this general rule occurs in Bob Jones' sixth-grade social studies textbook. Descriptions of contemporary life in European countries that are primarily Roman Catholic frequently include derogatory statements about the Church. "Almost all the children of [the Republic of] Ireland grow up believing in the traditions of the Roman Catholic church without knowing of God's free salvation."[6] After students read that "over ninety percent of the [Austrian] people are Roman Catholic,"[7] the text goes on to state:

> The Austrian people are very religious. They believe in God. They know of Christ and His good life. But they do not know that Christ died to save them from judgment and eternal death. They believe that their religious works will get them to heaven. Few missionaries are in Austria to tell the people about the salvation God has provided through Christ Jesus. Those people need to be shown the peace and the joy that they can have in their hearts when they accept Christ as their savior.[8]

When the students read about Spain, they are told, "Today almost all the people of Spain are Roman Catholic. They know the traditions of the church, but they do not know the way of true salvation."[9]

Before beginning the discussion of anti-Catholic bias, it is important to remind readers that the vast majority of textual material is not controversial. Like secular textbooks used in public schools, nonreligious private schools, and the majority of religious private schools, there are discussions of the prime meridian, Shakespeare, the Battle of the Bulge, Chinese art, the Great Barrier Reef, and so forth. On the other hand, the examples of anti-Catholic bias described in this chapter are only a small percentage of the total amount of material that denigrates the religion of approximately 60 million Americans. Furthermore, Roman Catholicism is not the only religion that is denigrated. Orthodox churches, many Protestant denominations, and virtually every non-Christian religion (with the exception of Judaism, though in some rare instances Judaism also is treated disrespectfully) that is mentioned or discussed in these texts are treated in ways that are substantially similar to the authors' treatment of Roman Catholicism.

Explicit Bias

In this chapter "explicit bias" means statements that are derogatory to Roman Catholicism or to members of the Roman

Catholic faith. For example, when the authors of A Beka's high school text ask students to "name two groups in Europe that stood for the Word of God against the Church of Rome?" in a chapter review question, they clearly imply that Roman Catholicism is outside the "Word of God."[10] The author of Bob Jones' high school text writes, "The seeds of error that took root during the fourth and fifth centuries blossomed into the Roman Catholic church — a perversion of biblical Christianity."[11] The same author describes the Roman Catholic Church as "the mixed offspring of biblical truth and pagan error."[12] These are direct statements that impugn the character of the Catholic Church and the religious faith of its adherents.

In A Beka's textbooks, explicit denigration of Roman Catholicism begins with the publisher's fifth-grade world history textbook. Much of this denigration is accomplished through the use of derogatory language, for example, the use of the word *distorted* and its variants. A Beka's seventh-grade world history book begins to use the terms *distorted* (*distort, distortion*), *false*, and *error* to refer to Roman Catholicism.[13] Indeed, the third unit of the text is titled "The Middle Ages and the Distortion of Christianity (A.D. 100-1500): Response to Christ." The early Roman church (before 500 A.D.) is described as "a monstrous distortion of Biblical Christianity."[14] Combee distinguishes the *invisible* church made up of "all true Christians" from the *visible* church of Rome: "The visible catholic church soon began to distort Christianity."[15] Speaking of the Crusades, he speculates that "if Christendom had succeeded with its crusades, distorted Christianity might have been imposed on all mankind."[16] "During the Middle Ages, the majority of Europeans were ruled by a religion that still called itself Christianity, but it was a distorted Christianity that had largely departed from the teachings of the Bible."[17] In the chapter titled "The Age of Darkness," which is subtitled "Distorted Christianity, Holy Roman Empire, Renaissance," the author writes, "The papacy had always distorted Christianity."[18] The publisher's 10th-grade world history book continues the use of these terms. For example, in explaining the growth of sacramental ritual, the authors state, "These errors and distortions [described as "elaborate rites and ceremonies with all the trappings of heathen temple worship" and attributed to the influence of paganism] grew into the false teachings and practices of the medieval church."[19] The Eastern church "adopted much of the same distorted views and pagan influence" of the Western church.[20] In speaking of the sacraments of the Western church, Thompson and Combee state that "as the Roman church evolved, many fundamental doctrines were also distorted, including the doctrine of salvation" and that "though the Roman church had seriously distorted New Testament Christianity, there were still some both within and without the church who stood for the truth of salvation by grace through faith in Jesus Christ."[21] Over and over again the terms *distorted* and *distortion* are used, including but not limited to discussions of scholasticism, Thomas Aquinas, the lack of social and economic progress during the Middle Ages, the papacy, the Renaissance, Wycliffe's translation of the Bible, Erasmus, and, of course, Martin Luther. In all, the seventh-grade book uses the term *distorted* or its variants 28 times when discussing Roman Catholicism in the six chapters in which its discussions of the Roman Catholic faith are most concentrated: chapters covering early Christianity, the Middle Ages, the Reformation, and so on.[22] A unit summary, included in these pages, uses the term eight more times; an introductory section also included in these pages uses it once. In these same chapters the term *false* is used four times (and three additional times in the summary). *Error* is used once in these chapters. In the publisher's 10th-grade text, *distorted* or its variants are used 14 times, *false* is used seven times, and *error* is used twice in the five chapters covering the same subject matter.[23]

Bob Jones University's world history texts do not have a term as commonly used as A Beka's *distortion* or *distorted*. The closest these texts come to this rhetoric is the following statement: "Rome the church after the introduction of Christianity, gradually developed into a religious system (Roman Catholicism) that has perverted the truth of Christianity."[24]

Both the A Beka and Bob Jones books use the term *false* to describe the doctrines and beliefs of the Catholic Church and less frequently *error*. Although this language appears in A Beka's fifth-grade text ("false teachings and practices"), it is more frequently used in the secondary texts.[25] Machiavelli "realized that further political progress would not be possible until men's minds were freed from false religion."[26] Even A Beka's 11th-grade U.S. history book repeats the characterization of Roman Catholicism as "false": "As others began studying the Scriptures for themselves, their eyes were opened to the false teachings of the Roman church, and they began to see the importance of a personal relationship with God. The Reformation soon spread throughout Europe bringing a *revival of Biblical Christianity*, which had been suppressed though never completely destroyed by leaders of the Roman church throughout the Middle Ages (emphasis in the original)."[27] Wycliffe and Huss "boldly opposed the errors of Roman Catholicism."[28] Tenth-graders using A Beka books are taught that "the doctrines and practices of the Roman church had digressed so far from Scripture that the church was compelled to keep its members from reading the Bible and discovering the truth."[29] "The common people [of the Middle Ages] lived under such spiritual bondage. Against this backdrop burst the Protestant Reformation, a movement that rediscovered Biblical truth."[30] A School of Tomorrow/Accelerated Christian Education booklet addresses the issues raised by the precursors to and leaders of the Reformation by explaining that:

> the Roman Catholic Church had absorbed non-Biblical doctrines concerning salvation and the authority of the church. Various works such as baptism, taking Communion, and doing penance were considered by many as necessary for salvation. The church had come to equate church authority with the Bible. The men we are going to study had come to know that salvation is from simple trust in Jesus Christ and not through works of any kind. They had come to see salvation as the work of God based upon the Death and Resurrection of Jesus Christ.[31]

A number of Roman Catholic doctrines or practices are criticized across grade levels in at least two of the three publishers' materials. All three publishers' materials disparage the doctrine of Apostolic succession. Fifth-graders are told, "Some men made themselves into gods by blocking the direct access to the Father through Jesus the Son. Men who said they were successors of the Apostles claimed, as no Apostle ever had, to be necessary for salvation."[32] In the seventh-grade text, the language becomes a little more explicit: "False beliefs about salvation led many to obey a few men who, with Christ in Heaven and not yet returned to visibly govern an earthly kingdom, took it upon themselves to rule the world in His name."[33] "The Peterine theory gave rise to the idea of the *Roman Catholic Church* [and] the bishop of Rome came to be called the *pope* (Latin, papa, meaning "father") and to be revered for his position in spite of Christ's instructions against such practices (Matt. 23:8-12)."[34] Medieval "people . . . looked up to the pope because they believed his false claim to be Christ's representative on earth as the successor of Peter."[35] "According to this theory, Peter supposedly became the vicar, or substitute, of Christ on earth. . . . The Peterine theory rests upon a number of false assumptions. . . . Another false assumption is that Peter, as the first pope, passed down his authority to succeeding bishops of Rome."[36] Describing Valla's assertion that the Donation of Constantine was a "forgery," the School of Tomorrow's booklet, *Renaissance and Reformation,* states, "This means that the papal claims to be supreme authority in the West were not valid. These claims of the Pope had been put forth for over 1,000 years!"[37]

The authors also denigrate the sacraments and the veneration of Mary and the saints. In A Beka's seventh-grade world history book, Combee writes, "Men had distorted baptism, making it an act necessary for salvation."[38] In another section he opines that "the Roman church encouraged prayer, but it was the wrong kind of prayer, addressed to the wrong people."[39] After discussing the Latin mass and the doctrine of transubstantiation, Combee states, in a section titled "The Virgin Mary, Saints, and Priests," that "the people followed many other false doctrines."[40] In the 10th-grade book students are asked, "How does [the dogma of transubstanti-ation] compare to the Biblical teaching about the Lord's Supper?" and are told that in the Middle Ages "men believed that the priests with their sacraments, not Christ with His grace, held the keys to the Heaven."[41] "Gradually, worship services became more and more complicated with ceremonies and rituals, and the churches began to accept false doctrines as well. What Satan could not achieve from without through persecution, he achieved from within through infiltration."[42] "The demands [of the Catholic church] led the people to regard Christ as a stern and merciless Judge" which led to their seeking the intercession of the Virgin Mary.[43] However, because "even Mary seemed unap-proachable, they also prayed to the long-departed apostles and other saints . . . but the Bible clearly teaches that there is only one mediator between God and man, Jesus Christ (1 Tim. 2:5)."[44]

The sacraments and veneration of the saints fare no better in the Bob Jones textbooks. To Fisher, "The doctrine and practice of the Roman church was a dangerous mix of truth and error."[45] By using the adverb *supposedly*, he, like the A Beka authors, casts aspersions on Roman Catholic sacraments: "During the [Euchar-ist], known as the mass, the priest supposedly transforms the bread and wine into the actual body and blood of Christ. This miraculous change is known as transubstantiation."[46] Indeed, all the sacraments are biblically unsound. "The words of Jesus Christ show the error of the [sacramental] system."[47] Fisher also states that the veneration of saints was "one of the greatest errors of the Roman church."[48]

Fifth-graders in schools that use A Beka textbooks are taught that although the monks were responsible for the preservation of the Bible, "many monks and other church leaders led wicked lives [and] became rich."[49] "The Bible says that a person is saved by faith in Christ alone, but the people did not know this because most of them could not read and only the church leaders were allowed to have Bibles. The people wanted eternal life so much that they did whatever the monks and priests told them."[50] Seventh-graders are taught that "monasticism became the ideal of some who called themselves Christians" (this phrase is also used in A Beka's 10th-grade text) and that monastic celibacy and withdrawal from the world were spiritual errors because monasticism is "a false notion of how Christians ought to live."[51] The author opines that "the Bible says just the opposite [and] the monks fell into the trap prophesied by Saint Paul [by] 1 Tim. 4: 1-4" (scriptural quotation omitted).[52] The fact that the Church gained material wealth when people entered monasteries is pointed out to 10th-graders. Perhaps the most stinging indictment of monasticism is contained in Bob Jones' world history textbooks: "Monasticism is not of Christian origin nor biblically based but from the Eastern pagan religions."[53] Subsequently, the author, as with the School of Tomorrow/Accelerated Christian Education booklet that covers the Middle Ages, gives credit to the monks for preserving the Bible.

Discussions of medieval religious dissenters and leaders of the Reformation are used to make statements that emphasize the alleged weaknesses and falsity of Roman Catholicism. Fifthgraders are taught that "some people during the Middle Ages did not believe all the teachings of the monks, priests, and popes. . . . *Peter of Bruis* read the Bible and became a true Christian."[54] Speaking of Martin Luther, A Beka's fifth-grade social studies book describes his conversion: "Not by works, but by faith he came to Christ and knew that he was saved."[55] "Brav[ely he] challeng[ed] the false but very powerful Roman church."[56] Seventhgraders are introduced to the obscure theologian, Marsilius of Padua: "During the Middle Ages, the unscriptural doctrines of the Roman church did not go completely unchallenged. . . . Relying on the Bible, Marsilius rejected one Roman doctrine after another — including the opinion that without forgiveness by a priest, God's grace is insufficient to save a person from sin."[57] Moving to the Reformation, the author states, "Luther was now able to see through many of the false beliefs and practices of the Roman church."[58] Somewhat archly, groups that the Roman Catholic Church regarded as heretics are denominated as "Christians Outside the Church of Rome."[59] The authors of the 10th-grade text include the Petrobrusians and Waldensians and their founders among the "many brave individuals and groups [who] stood alone for the truths of the Scriptures even when the church as a whole departed from Biblical Christianity."[60] Turning to the Reformation, the authors find Luther a heroic figure who "hurled the Biblical teaching that as far as God is concerned, all believers are priests" against the "wall" of Catholic ecclesiastical organization.[61]

Readers are most likely to have encountered the term *Romanism* in their study of American history. The term was part of the "Rum, Romanism, and Rebellion" campaign slogan of Grover Cleveland's 1884 presidential campaign. *Romanism* and *Romanist* are derogatory terms when applied to the Roman Catholic Church or adherents of the Church.[62] A Beka books use these terms repeatedly, especially in the publisher's 10th-grade world history books. In the seventh-grade text, Combee states that "by the eleventh century Catholic missionaries were working in Scandinavia [and] many Scandinavians embraced Romanism."[63] The 10th-grade book uses the term *Romanism* or a variant 32 times when discussing Roman Catholicism in the five chapters in which its discussions of the Church are most concentrated, that is, chapters covering the Middle Ages, the Reformation, and the Counter-Reformation and post-Reformation period.[64] The Bob Jones texts also use *Romanism* or its derivatives, though they do so relatively infrequently compared to the A Beka texts and School of Tomorrow/Accelerated Christian Education materials. For example, English Puritans wanted to "rid England of Romanist influences."[65] "Most Protestants in the [American] colonies feared Roman Catholicism. Some of this feeling was simple prejudice, but much of it resulted from opposition to the un-Biblical teachings of the Roman Catholic church and from Romanist repression of Protestantism in Catholic countries."[66] It is possible the authors are unaware of the pejorative connotation of these terms. They might consider them the equivalent of Protestantism and Lutheranism; however, this explanation seems unlikely because the authors are historians, appear to have a command of religious history, and make numerous negative statements about Roman Catholicism.[67]

Implicit Bias

It is axiomatic that it is far more difficult, if not virtually impossible, to prove the negative because it is more difficult to describe the absence of something than its presence. The absence of content is far less apparent than statements that explicitly denigrate Roman Catholicism. However, exclusion is a subtle but powerful mechanism for marginalizing and encouraging hostility toward certain groups. It could be argued that these books do include Roman Catholics and discuss the Roman Catholic Church; but in four instances, absence of certain material serves to magnify the effect of the explicit bias I have just discussed. Moreover, the implicit bias that I take up in the following sections is mixed with and magnified by explicit bias in the form of derogatory statements.

First, Catholics and the Catholic Church are rarely called "Christian." Second, these texts describe in detail and at great length the Catholic persecution of Protestants; but, almost without exception, the Protestant persecution of Catholics is omitted. Third, Catholic figures who have been important figures in world history are discussed in ways that vary considerably from texts commonly used in public schools. Reference to their Catholicism is omitted, downplayed, or called into question. The coverage given to them or their accomplishments often is considerably less robust than that given to less important historical figures. Fourth, Protestant missionary activities are extensively discussed in highly approving tones, while Catholic missionary efforts are seldom mentioned.

The most basic of the implicit anti-Catholic biases is a noticeable avoidance of using the word *Christian* in reference to Roman Catholics or the Catholic Church in A Beka's textbooks and to a somewhat lesser extent in the Bob Jones and School of Tomorrow materials. In the A Beka texts, when the word *Christianity* is used to refer to the Roman Catholic Church or its teachings, it frequently is used with the adjective *distorted*. In addition, the texts seem to avoid using *Roman* and *Catholic* together.

Consistently, the Roman Catholic Church is referred to as the "Roman church" or the "Church of Rome," though on rare occasions Catholics are called Christians and the church is called the "Roman Catholic Church," as when contemporary Rome is identified as the "headquarters of the Roman Catholic Church."[68] A Beka books frequently use the term *Christendom*, defined as "the nations who professed to be Christian," to refer to medieval Western Europe.[69] This phraseology avoids the necessity of applying the term *Christianity* to the Roman Catholic Church or using such expressions as "the medieval church" or even just "the Church" as alternate or shorthand ways of referring to Roman Catholicism. Medieval groups who challenged the Roman Catholic Church are repeatedly referred to as "Christians," and there are many references to "true Christians," "Bible believing Christians," and "believing Christians." For example, the author of A Beka's seventh-grade world history text writes, "Through the ages, true Christians have shared the conviction that the Bible is the inspired Word of God and the rule of faith and practice for all believers."[70] Speaking of the followers of John Huss, the same text states that "a movement for true Christianity broke out in the country of Bohemia."[71] In a section titled "Christian Heroes," fifth-graders are told that Peter Waldo, a medieval opponent of Roman Catholicism, is "another Christian hero" (this language follows a paragraph discussing Peter of Bruis, another religious reformer).[72] The discussion of Peter of Bruis and Peter Waldo and their followers, "these brave Christians" (also described as "heroic Christians") in A Beka's 10th-grade text is placed in a large highlighted box titled "Christians Outside the Church of Rome."[73] Peter of Bruis "rejected the Roman Church in favor of God's Word," and Peter Waldo is described as coming "to the conviction that Scripture is the sole authority for Christians."[74] At the end of their discussion of Protestant reformers, Thompson and Combee move their discussion from the historical by noting that "over the centuries many Christians . . . have considered themselves '*Calvinists*'" (emphasis in the original).[75] No one would consider Catholics to be included in a group of Calvinistic denominations;

but by not using the terms *Protestant* and *Protestants*, the authors subtly affirm Catholicism's place *outside* the community of Christian churches.

Bob Jones' high school history book also gives the Waldensians a highlighted box. The first sentence reads, "The increasing corruption of the medieval church was not unnoticed by Christians."[76] Perhaps the most striking example of this reluctance to include Roman Catholics in the family of Christians occurs not in a discussion of medieval dissenters but in a description of Chinese victims of the Boxer Rebellion of 1900. Tenth-graders read that "over a thousand Chinese Protestants and an untold number of Chinese Catholics were . . . murdered."[77] As in some Southern cemeteries where whites and African Americans do not lie next to each other, so too Protestants and Catholics are not joined together as victims of a massacre.

The School of Tomorrow materials are more likely to apply the term *Christian* to the Catholic church. For example, "Clovis also was converted to Catholic Christianity from paganism."[78] On the other hand, a different booklet states, "In spite of his lip service to Roman Catholicism and his probably [sic] Jewish background, Christopher Columbus was very possibly a secret Christian."[79]

Religious Persecution

Many instances of Catholic persecution of Protestants are described, and some of these descriptions include gratuitous detail regarding the form of the persecution. There is no attempt to place these graphic details in the context of the extreme cruelty that characterized medieval culture. Hanging, disemboweling, and quartering were common methods of execution. Torture was used extensively in the legal system. The materials fail to include the torture and execution of many thousands of accused witches by both Catholics and Protestants. A student relying on these texts for his or her understanding of history would, understandably, conclude that during the Middle Ages and the Reformation and its aftermath, only the Roman Catholic church engaged in religious violence and persecution. Great attention is paid to the

Inquisition, and in some cases specific Catholic orders are linked to religious persecution.

As with other examples of anti-Catholic bias, this portrayal of religious persecution as almost exclusively perpetrated by Catholics starts relatively mildly in A Beka's elementary world history text: "The church [the preceding sentence uses the term 'Roman church'] set up a special court called the Inquisition which they [sic] used to find heretics and kill them if they would not renounce their faith in Christ."[80] The seventh-grade A Beka text gives the Inquisition a highlighted text box that includes the following, more detailed information: "Most of those condemned to death were burned at stake; others were beaten to death or drowned."[81] "The bloodshed continued throughout the 1400s and into the 1500s and 1600s. The Inquisition was called the sanctum officium (Holy Office) because the church considered its work so praiseworthy."[82] The 10th-grade text states: "The Franciscans and Dominicans . . . were largely responsible for conducting the merciless persecution of those who opposed the Roman church."[83]

The gratuitous details in the discussions of Catholic persecution of Protestants include descriptions of the sufferings of both individual martyrs and victimized groups. Following are a few examples:

- Peter of Bruis "burned at the stake for his faith."[84]
- John Huss "burned at the stake"[85] (*"burned him at the stake*,"[86] "the burning of Huss,"[87] "burned at the stake"[88]). In the seventh-grade text, Combee includes a color picture of the execution of Huss and describes it in detail (the placing of a paper crown on Huss' head and his response to this indignity). Huss' dying words are included in several of these books. Bob Jones' 10th-grade textbook both quotes his dying words and describes his execution ("the flames ended his earthly life") in some detail.[89] Huss' martyrdom also is described in the Bob Jones U.S. history book: "burned at the stake in 1415 for rejecting Roman Catholic teachings."[90]

- Wycliffe was "harassed . . . until his death." "The pope commanded that Wycliffe's remains be dug up and burned."[91] "At the pope's command Wycliffe's remains were dug up and burned."[92] The Church "harassed him for his remaining years."[93] "The pope commanded that Wycliffe's bones be dug up and burned."[94] "Forty-four years after his death, Wycliffe's bones were dug up and burned. His ashes were thrown into a nearby stream."[95]

- Tyndale, who was "strangled and burned at the stake . . . died a martyr's death"[96] ("strangled and then burned at the stake"[97]). An illustration of the execution appears in A Beka's English literature book (see discussion of Fox's *Book of Martyrs* below). Tyndale's execution also is included in Bob Jones' high school U.S. history book, "strangled and burned at the stake by Catholics."[98]

- Anglican Bishops Lattimer, Ridley, and Cranmer were "burned at the stake."[99] Lattimer's dying words are quoted, and Fox's *Book of Martyrs* is mentioned. "As the fire was lit, Lattimer said to Ridley . . ."[100] The heroism of Archbishop Cranmer also is described: "As the flames came up about [Cranmer], he thrust [his] hand into the fire."[101] Keesee and Sidwell include a rather gruesome woodcut from Fox's *Book of Martyrs* in Bob Jones' history book.

Both A Beka's and Bob Jones' high school English books contain multipage excerpts from the *Book of Martyrs*. A Beka's *Introduction to English Literature* excerpt describing the death of Dr. Rowland Taylor concludes with: "Soyce with a halbert struck him on the head that the brains fell out, and the corpse fell into the fire."[102] A woodcut showing Tyndale bound to the stake with chains also appears on this page. Bob Jones' *British Literature for Christian Schools* also reproduces an excerpt from Fox describing the deaths of Lattimer, Ridley, and Cranmer. Ridley's death is described in excruciating detail: "The fire . . . burned clean all his nether parts before it once touched the upper; and that made him leap up and down under the faggots and often desire them to let the fire come unto him, saying, 'I cannot burn'."[103] Finally, a bystander pulled back the faggots with a staff and Ridley seeing "the fire flame up . . . wrestled himself unto that side . . . falling down at master Lattimer's feet."[104] This section includes a woodcut showing Lattimer and Ridley bound to the stake with wood piled around them. Not one book mentions that Roman Catholic Bishop John Fisher also was burned at the stake in Tudor England for his faith.

The texts also include information about the persecution of religious groups that challenged the Roman Catholic church. Fifth-grade students using A Beka texts are introduced to this subject when they read that the followers of Wycliffe (Lollards) suffered "terrible persecution" and that the Dutch lived in "great fear of the *Spanish Inquisition*, which tortured people to try to force them to follow the pope."[105] Both seventh- and 10th-graders also read about the abuses of the Inquisition: "Throughout Europe, particularly in Italy and Spain, the Inquisition *used torture and terror to obtain confessions of heresy* for its Protestant victims (emphasis in the original)."[106] "About 8,000 people were executed" by "what came to he known as the Council of Blood" convened by the Spanish Duke of Alva.[107]

Concerning the persecution of French Huguenots, fifth-grade students are told that "France lost its chance to become a nation blessed by God" because of its "terrible persecution" of the Huguenots "for their faith."[108] ". . . perhaps as many as 100,000 [French Protestant] Huguenots were murdered" in the aftermath of the St. Bartholomew's Day Massacre.[109] King Charles IX is described as "raving like a maniac [as he] burst out, 'Kill the admiral, if you like but kill all the Huguenots with him — all — all — all — all. . . . See to it at once — at once; do you hear?'" (ellipsis in the original).[110] Tenth-grade students are told, "In Rome a medal was struck to commemorate the massacre, and rousing songs of thanksgiving were sung."[111]

Students using A Beka's 10th-grade world history book read about the Catholic Mary Tudor's persecutions of English Protestants ("about 300 persons who refused to obey 'Bloody

Mary' . . . died for their convictions") and students learn that "the *Scottish Reformation* opened violently with execution of preachers who urged reform" (emphases in the original).[112] The authors also include two illustrations showing victims of the Inquisition being tortured by the rack and strappado. Inquisitors "might pull his bones out of joint or burn various parts of his body."[113] In France "bands of Roman Catholics began roving the city, breaking into homes and murdering their unsuspecting and helpless occupants."[114] Fisher acknowledges that "by the nineteenth century, the Inquisition finally stopped its bloody activities, but the organization itself continued. Today it is called the Sacred Congregation for the Doctrine of the Faith."[115]Acknowledgment that cruelty existed on both sides, when it comes, is scanty and so oblique as to fail entirely to balance the accounts of Catholic excesses. "The modern student might well ask, why did Catholics and Protestants kill each other . . . ?"[116] Even when persecution by Protestants is explicitly mentioned, it is intra-Protestant violence to which students are exposed. "Certain Lutheran rulers persecuted Anabaptists."[117]

School of Tomorrow/Accelerated Christian Education materials are not nearly as detailed as those published by A Beka and Bob Jones. For example, "Charles V and Phillip II [of Spain attempted] to force the Dutch to become Catholic again."[118] Mary Tudor "had about three hundred [Protestants] killed and many others were forced to flee for their lives."[119] "Her rampages against Protestants earned her the title of 'Bloody Mary.'"[120] The persecution of the Huguenots is described as "one of the great errors in judgment of Louis XIV."[121]

Notable Catholic Figures in History. Roman Catholicism is stripped of one of its most affectionately regarded heroes. In A Beka's senior high school world history text, students read about St. Patrick in a large highlighted text box, titled "Patrick of Ireland." The denial of the Patrick's link to the Church occurs at the end of this material: "Although the Roman church later claimed Patrick as her own, calling him 'Saint Patrick' and 'patron saint of Ireland,' Patrick had no connection with the Roman church or the pope. In fact, Romanism was not even introduced to the British Isles until the seventh century."[122]

Thomas á Becket is mentioned only in the publisher's 10th-grade text. The approach is factual, though the text omits any reference to reverence given to Becket after his murder by Henry II's knights. In the Bob Jones student text, Becket's conflict with Henry II is described and students learn that "Becket became a martyr and his tomb a popular shrine."[123] The teacher's notes, however, reveal a different view of the archbishop. "Becket was a consummate actor . . . and it is uncertain whether he really believed that he was doing God's will or whether he was determined to play the part of the archbishop to the end."[124]

Thomas Aquinas is contrasted unfavorably with other medieval theologians, such as Anselm, Peter Abelard, and William Ockham. "His philosophy, called Thomism . . . denied the totality of man's sinful nature and his dependence upon God for everything. Greatly impressed by Thomism because it stressed man's self-salvation through works, the Roman church gave it official approval and forbade anyone to disagree; consequently, progress in philosophy and science became virtually impossible under such conditions."[125] Aquinas receives a more measured consideration by Fisher; however, the Bob Jones text goes on to point out the weaknesses of scholasticism on spiritual grounds. "[The scholastics'] attempt to apply human reasoning to spiritual truth often led them into error."[126] "Many contradictions [revealed by the scholastics] were not contradictions in Scripture but in the fallible decrees of popes. . . . In this way God used the scholastics to prepare for the coming of the Reformation — a period in which men once again recognized the Bible as the only infallible source of truth."[127]

Like other topics, A Beka's coverage of the life of Joan of Arc is more positive at the elementary level. Joan is described as a "young peasant girl" who helped the French defeat the English and who was "burned at the stake."[128] For seventh- and 10th-graders the coverage of Joan changes to the following statement:

"One of the weakest French kings allowed Joan of Arc, a peasant girl who claimed to hear 'heavenly voices,' to lead the French army into battle. Surprisingly, the 'Maid of Orleans' did win a few victories, but they proved to be temporary. Joan was captured and executed by the English."[129] Joan of Arc was burned at the stake; however, unlike the Protestant martyrs, Ridley, Lattimer, and Cranmer, her suffering is not described in A Beka world history textbooks. Fisher gives Joan a bit more credit for her influence in reviving French nationalism, mentions that she was burned at the stake, and includes a picture of her riding through a French town. The School of Tomorrow/Accelerated Christian Education materials do not mention Joan; but given the overall scantiness of their coverage of a variety of topics, this in itself is not surprising.

The School of Tomorrow/Accelerated Christian Education high school materials treat Columbus and the discovery of the New World in a fashion that is quite different from that of textbooks used in public schools and, indeed, from the A Beka and Bob Jones texts. For example, Grussendorf, Lowman, and Ashbaugh, the authors of A Beka's junior high school American history textbook, describe Columbus as a "devout Catholic."[130] The School of Tomorrow/Accelerated Christian Education's coverage of Columbus begins with a detailed description of pre-Columbian voyages to the New World, for example, Welsh and Irish monks (identified as "not Roman Catholic"), several Viking explorers, Prince Madoc of Wales ("the supposed voyage of Prince Madoc . . ."), Antonio Zeno, and Joao Vas Corte Real.[131] In all, 133 lines of text (excluding text review questions) discuss these early voyages of discovery. The booklet describes in some detail the family relationships that would have made Columbus aware of Real's voyage and comments that Columbus "must have been" aware of the Viking sagas and that "it would have been next to impossible for Columbus . . . to have been in ignorance of these tales. . . ."[132]

One hundred and thirty-two lines (excluding text review questions) are devoted to Columbus and his discovery and exploration of the New World; however, 34 lines are devoted to establishing the possibility that Columbus was a "clandestine Sephardic Jew."[133] Not all the statements assert this hypothesis; some serve to establish an argument leading to this conclusion. This section includes a one-paragraph description of early Spanish history before the Inquisition and such statements as "for some unknown reason, all records of [Columbus'] birth and baptism were destroyed by the Jesuit Order" and "in Spain the navigator called himself Colon [which was] a popular Sephardic Jewish name."[134] Columbus' religious beliefs and motivation are given fairly extensive coverage. This material includes two statements that link his putative Jewish background and the assertion that he was not truly Roman Catholic. Columbus "was apparently a nominal practicing Roman Catholic in Catholic Italy and Spain [who gave] lip service to Roman Catholicism."[135] Taken as a whole, this material undercuts both the significance of Columbus' discovery of the New World and his status as a Roman Catholic, in part because the space (lines of text) given to the pre-Columbian explorations outweighs that given to Columbus' voyages when the material devoted to his religion is subtracted.

Thomas More, a Catholic lawyer, was executed for his opposition to Henry VIII's break with the Roman Catholic Church. The authors of A Beka's high school world history text describe his adherence to his faith in negative terms. "Although More never joined the Protestant Reformation, he urged the church to reform the clergy and correct certain doctrines."[136] Thus students might well infer that More might have been a secret Protestant or at least have had sympathy with the reformers and might have joined the Reformation had he lived. More, one of Catholicism's staunchest defenders and a person whose courage has resonated for almost five hundred years, is robbed of the convictions for which he died. By emphasizing his criticisms of his beloved church, his martyrdom is diminished.

Missionary Activity. Discussions of Protestant missionaries almost inevitably include praise for their motives, character, and courage. In the few instances in which Catholic missionaries are mentioned, their motives, almost without exception, are disparaged. Eighth-graders using A Beka's U.S. history text learn only that "[some] Spanish settlements began as missions to the Indians" and that "Jacques Marquette [was] a Jesuit missionary."[137] Tenth-graders read that Spanish explorers of the New World hoped to "spread Romanism (by force, if necessary) among the native inhabitants."[138] Eleventh-graders receive a less pejorative view. "[The Spanish] introduced Catholicism which is still dominant in Latin America . . . and established many Catholic missions."[139] Tenth-graders using Bob Jones' world history text are told, "Not all of Europe's religious zeal was directed against the Muslims. Some explorers went out seeking to spread the gospel to heathen people, who needed to hear of salvation in Jesus Christ alone. Unfortunately, most of the early explorers were Roman Catholics. Instead of leading people to Christ, they won converts to the Roman Catholic church."[140] Later the author writes, "[Roman Catholic] evangelistic efforts [in Central and South America made] a mockery of the gospel."[141] Eleventh-graders learning American history by reading the publisher's textbook learn that "most Protestants in the [American] colonies feared Roman Catholicism. Some of this feeling was simple prejudice, but much of it resulted from opposition to the un-Biblical teachings of the Roman Catholic church and from Romanist repression of Protestantism in Catholic countries . . . these powers were not above using Catholic priests and missionaries to achieve their political goals."[142] The authors describe the influence of religion on the encomida system of Spanish Central and South America by writing that "the Catholic religion that the Spanish brought with them reinforced rather than reduced these authoritarian tendencies."[143]

Discussing the Mogul period of Indian history, a School of Tomorrow booklet tells students, "Christians went to present Christ and his teachings. The Jesuits went to present their version of Christianity, but Akbar was not too impressed — especially with the worship of saints and great veneration of Mary. Akbar never became a Christian, perhaps because his view of Christianity was not a true one."[144] Turning to Spanish colonization of Central and South America, *The Age of Exploration*, a School of Tomorrow/Accelerated Christian Education booklet, states, "It was the duty of ['the conquistadors and padres'] to spread Christianity and civilization among the pagan inhabitants of the Americas, but this they failed to do. By means of the sword, thousands upon thousands of unbelieving Indians were forced to accept the Catholic baptism of sprinkled 'holy water.' The result was not converted Indians but merely thousands upon thousands of slightly damp but still unbelieving natives. Very rarely, indeed, did these lost heathen have the true Gospel of Christ preached to them."[145] Although Catholic missionary activities during the colonial period are given scanty and divided coverage, the School of Tomorrow/Accelerated Christian Education booklet that covers contemporary history devotes seven paragraphs (in a section titled, "Spiritual Awakening: Latin America") to a discussion of contemporary Protestant evangelism in Latin America[146] and describes missionary activities in five countries (Brazil, Chile, El Salvador, Guatemala, and Mexico) and among the Quechera Indians.

One aspect of these texts that reflects their religious orientation is the inclusion of faith-based missionary activities. Typically, public school students would encounter missionaries in a more distant, historical, and — though it is somewhat odd to describe it in this fashion — secular context, for example, French and Spanish missionary activities in the New World. Readers who grew up with the Catholic textbooks once used in parochial schools learned about Roman Catholic missionaries and might not have encountered any Protestant missionaries, other than Dr. David Livingston. Similarly, fundamentalist Christian textbooks introduce students to many evangelical Protestant missionaries but few Catholic ones. In A Beka's fifth-grade world history textbook, a fair amount of space is devoted to these individuals and their missionary activities. Missions to Africa encompass several pages, including a two-page, highlighted text box that praises

Mary Slessor, "Queen of the Cannibals."[147] The authors briefly mention missions to native people in Australia and New Zealand and give John G. Patton, a missionary to the Pacific island of Aniwa, coverage in a text box. Missions to China include descriptions of the evangelicalism of Hudson Taylor and John and Betty Stam. A full-page highlighted text box of 81 lines discusses William Carey's mission to India. A two-page highlighted text box features "Amy Carmichael: Rescuer of Indian Children."[148]

Although no fewer than 550 lines are devoted to missionaries ministering to Third World peoples, Mother Theresa is not mentioned. While the coverage of evangelical Protestant missionaries varies from book to book, the omission of any mention of Mother Theresa is a constant. Of course, these are religious textbooks and one would expect a considerable amount of attention to Protestant missionaries and their activities. But the question is not whether such materials ought to include this kind of coverage; it is whether the public should subsidize their dissemination. This is not an argument for some type of balanced treatment, but whether the opt-out provisions in current voucher programs are or could be adequate. Finally, the broadest and perhaps most troubling question is the effect of the unbalanced coverage (again understandable and beyond question permissible) in sectarian school textbooks with the texts' unequivocal and explicit animus toward Roman Catholicism.

The lack of balanced coverage extends beyond Protestant and Catholic missionary activity. Just as Mother Theresa is absent from all texts, the influence of Pope John Paul II in bringing freedom to the people of Poland and Eastern Europe is barely mentioned or omitted entirely. This is all the more striking because all the texts give considerable coverage to the evils of Communism and, by implication, the desirability of ending Communist regimes. In A Beka's 11th-grade world history text, Pope John Paul II's support for Solidarity is given one sentence. In the comparable Bob Jones text, Solidarity is mentioned, but the role of the Roman Catholic Church is not. In discussing resistance to the

Communist government of Poland during the 1980s, School of Tomorrow/Accelerated Christian Education materials state that "Solidarity had become (along with the Polish Church and the Communist Party) one of the three great powers within Poland."[149] The Polish Church is not identified as Roman Catholic. Nowhere in the publisher's materials is Pope John Paul II or the Catholic Church mentioned as instrumental in the overthrow of Poland's communist regime. By contrast, the role of a Protestant minister, "Pastor Lazlo Tokes" of the Hungarian Reformed Church, in the resistance to the Nicolae Ceausescu's communist government is discussed in great detail.[150] Of the 44 lines of text devoted to the overthrow of the communist regime in Romania, 35 discuss Toke's role.

Concluding Comments

Sadly, the United States has a well-documented history of anti-Catholicism.[151] Unlike the Nativist movement, which combined anti-Catholic with ethnic prejudice, the A Beka, Bob Jones, and Accelerated Christian Education materials express an antipathy based solely on religion.

Contemporary manifestations of anti-Catholicism are not difficult to find; and, like the materials in the A Beka, Bob Jones, and Accelerated Christian Education texts, they decouple religious and ethnic animus.[152] In a 2001 Pew Charitable Trust survey, 13% of the respondents indicated that they had a unfavorable or very unfavorable opinion of Roman Catholics.[153] Writing about the 1997 controversy over the posting of the Ten Commandments in an Alabama courtroom, Lubet characterizes the following quotations from a 1947 book as "virulent anti-Catholicism."[154] "Catholics not only make 'graven images' in direct prohibition and violation of the Second Commandment, but they also worship these images in defiance of an angry and vengeful God."[155] Lubet goes on to note that the author describes the Ten Commandments as promulgated by the Catholic Church as "a mutilated set of Commandments."[156] "Mutilated" is not far from the language employing such words as "perverted" and "distorted" used in Christian school textbooks today.

Arguing that one of the primary purposes of democratic education is to inculcate in its future citizens the value of religious tolerance, Gutmann recognizes that "many . . . parents, although less radical in their rejection of modern society [than Old Order Amish], are committed to teaching their children religious and racial intolerance."[157] And she acknowledges that had American education been privatized during the 19th century, "the Protestant majority would have continued to educate their children [in separate Protestant schools] to be disrespectful if not intolerant of Catholics" with the result that anti-Catholic prejudice affecting the political, economic, and social well-being of Roman Catholics would have persisted until the present day.[158] In my opinion, Gutmann is entirely too sanguine about the dangers of the contemporary privatization movement and the issue of anti-Catholicism when she states that "there may be little reason today for Catholic parents to worry that privatizing schools will reinstitutionalize bigotry against Catholics."[159] To the contrary, the textbooks and materials published by A Beka, Bob Jones, and Accelerated Christian Education indicate that this is a very real possibility. Although I sometimes remark that the devil can cite anecdotes even as he can quote scripture, I recall a telephone call I received from a colleague who wondered if I could explain why students at a Christian school (that used A Beka textbooks) were taunting Roman Catholic children about their religion. I had no difficulty understanding at least some of the dynamics involved.

The curricular materials examined in this chapter and in Chapter Five raise a number of troubling issues. The first concerns the propriety of using tax funds under current and prospective voucher programs to support schools that base their curricula on these materials. This issue generates three questions:

- Whether we as a society wish the nation's children to be exposed to materials that denigrate the religious beliefs of other Americans.

- Whether we wish to support and encourage, through the use of public funds, the publication and dissemination of materials described in this chapter.
- Whether it is fair to require taxpayers to subsidize the purchase or teaching of materials that disparage their religion.

This last question is a particularly ironic one. Some conservative Protestant groups and individuals have alleged that the materials used in public schools disparage their religion, and it is true that textbooks used in public schools have tended to exclude coverage of religion generally. However, even though textbooks used in public schools tend to be weak in the area of religion, they do not systematically and pervasively combine omission with denigration of the most cherished and deeply held religious beliefs of any particular religious group or of religion in general.

The second major issue is more broadly political and philosophical. What might be the effect on our public life if a significant number of young people were exposed to these materials? That anti-Catholic bias is pervasive in these curricular materials is beyond question, though further study is warranted. It would be extremely difficult to assess the impact of these materials on the attitudes of children because conservative Protestants are extremely reluctant to allow their children to participate in studies designed to assess attitudes. Nevertheless, questions related to the exposure of future citizens to these materials are relevant to the current public debate over the privatization of American education and the proper role of the state in regulating home-schooling families. Scholars, policy makers, and members of the general public have long been silent on the issue of Christian school curricula.

At the most basic level lies the question of whether children exposed to such materials are being prepared to participate in a religiously diverse, representative democracy. When children from highly religious families, who presumably grow to adulthood continuing to believe in the preeminence of religious values, are taught that a group of their fellow Americans are believers in a "distorted" and "false" religion, can they as adults learn to respect and value those who belong to the disparaged faith? If they cannot, then how will they, as adults, treat their fellow Americans? If they are in positions of leadership, will they be able make decisions and policies that are fair? Will they be able to engage in a meaningful dialogue with members of a group they have been taught to despise? Will they be able to work for the honest consensus on which so much of our political life depends? Or will they be more likely to be either insincere or confrontational when they encounter others with whom they have profound religious differences?

For much, though not all, of our history, the United States has been spared the religious violence and strife that has plagued and continues to plague many other nations. What has allowed such a religiously diverse nation to exist relatively free of sectarian discord? To a large extent, the founders, so much closer than we to the horrors of the violence between Protestants and Catholics of the 14th, 15th, and 16th centuries, fashioned a nation in which religion and government were kept separate and religious liberty was a preeminent value. The separation of church and state, in turn, allowed for the eventual development of a system of education where the religious beliefs of some Americans might be neglected but would never be the subject of pervasive and systematic disparagement.

Notes

1. Ruth Miller Elson, *Guardians of Tradition: American Schoolbooks of the Nineteenth Century* (Lincoln: University of Nebraska Press, 1964), p. 53.
2. Ibid., p. 47, quoting J.A. Cummings, *An Introduction to Ancient and Modern Geography, on the Plan of Goldsmith and Guy* (Boston: Cummings and Hilliard, 1817), p. 168. Elson cites several other textbooks for this quotation.
3. Ibid., p. 47, quoting Daniel Adams, *The Monitorial Reader* (Concord, N.H.: Luther Roby, 1845), p. 146. Again, Elson cites a number of other textbooks for this quotation.
4. Ibid., pp. 41-42.

5. Raymond A. St. John, *American Literature for Christian Schools, Teacher's Edition* (Greenville, S.C.: Bob Jones University Press, 1994), p. 540.
6. *Heritage Studies for Christian Schools 6: Eastern Hemisphere Nations* (Greenville, S.C.: Bob Jones University Press, 1986), p. 41.
7. Ibid., p. 80.
8. Ibid.
9. Ibid., p. 94.
10. George Thompson and Jerry Combee, *World History and Cultures in Christian Perspective*, 2nd ed. (Pensacola, Fla.: A Beka, 1997), p. 170.
11. David A. Fisher, *World History for Christian Schools, Teacher's Edition*, 2nd ed. (Greenville, S.C.: Bob Jones University Press, 1994), p. 114.
12. Ibid., p. 179.
13. Jerry H. Combee, *History of the World in Christian Perspective, Teacher Edition*, 3rd ed. (Pensacola, Fla.: A Beka, 1995), pp. 426, 427, 420.
14. Ibid., p. 192.
15. Ibid., p. 138.
16. Ibid., p. 155.
17. Ibid., p. 199.
18. Ibid., p. 184.
19. Thompson and Combee, op. cit., p. 150.
20. Ibid., p. 157.
21. Ibid., pp. 165, 167.
22. Combee, op. cit., pp. 132-217.
23. Thompson and Combee, op. cit., pp. 140-255.
24. Fisher, op. cit., p. 73.
25. *Old World History*, p. 28.
26. Ibid., p. 188.
27. Michael Lowman, George Thompson, and Kurt Grussendorf, *United States History in Christian Perspective: Heritage of Freedom*, 2nd ed. (Pensacola, Fla.: A Beka, 1996), p. 9.
28. Fisher, p. 284.
29. Thompson and Combee, op. cit., p. 167.
30. Timothy Keesee and Mark Sidwell, *United States History for Christian Schools, Teacher's Edition*, 2nd ed. (Pensacola, Fla.: A Beka, 1991), p. 6.

31. *Renaissance and Reformation.* Self-Pac® of Basic Education (#103) (n.p.: Reform Publications, 1974), p. 15.

32. *Old World History*, pp. 144-45.

33. Combee, op. cit., p. 192.

34. Thompson and Combee, op. cit., p. 165.

35. Ibid., p. 181.

36. Fisher, op. cit., p. 181.

37. *Renaissance and Reformation*, p. 4.

38. Combee, op. cit., p. 145.

39. Ibid., p. 176.

40. Ibid., p. 177.

41. Thompson and Combee, op. cit., pp. 182, 189.

42. Ibid., p. 163.

43. Ibid., p. 167.

44. Ibid.

45. Fisher, op. cit., p. 182.

46. Ibid.

47. Ibid., p. 183.

48. Ibid., p. 181.

49. *Old World History*, p. 131.

50. Ibid.

51. Combee, op. cit., p. 175.

52. Ibid., p. 176.

53. Fisher, op. cit., p. 113.

54. *Old World History*, p. 132.

55. Ibid., p. 134.

56. Ibid.

57. Combee, op. cit., p. 140.

58. Ibid., p. 209.

59. Thompson and Combee, op. cit., p. 168.

60. Ibid.

61. Ibid., p. 249.

62. *New Shorter Oxford English Dictionary*, s.v. "Romanism." *The American Heritage Dictionary of the English Language, 4th ed.* describes "Romanism" as "offensive" (s.v. Romanism). *Merriam-Webster's Collegiate Dictionary* lists it as "often offensive" (s.v. "Romanism").

63. Combee, op. cit., p. 230.

64. Thompson and Combee, op. cit., pp. 162-281.
65. Keesee and Sidwell, op. cit., p. 22.
66. Ibid., p. 71.
67. For example, "Each prince would decide which religion, Romanism or Lutheranism, would be officially permitted and established in their territory." Combee, op. cit., p. 220.
68. *Old World History*, p. 157.
69. Lowman, Thompson, and Grussendorf, op. cit., p. 8; Kurt A. Grussendorf, Michael R. Lowman, and Brian S. Ashbaugh. *America: Land That I Love, Teacher Edition* (Pensacola, Fla.: A Beka, 1994), p. 5.
70. Combee, op. cit., p. 136.
71. Ibid., p. 204.
72. *Old World History*, p. 132.
73. Thompson and Combee, op. cit., p. 168.
74. Ibid.
75. Ibid., p. 254.
76. Fisher, op. cit., p. 249.
77. Thompson and Combee, op. cit., p. 52.
78. *Early Middle Ages.* Self-Pac® of Basic Education (#101), rev. 1995 (n.p.: Reform Publications, 1974), p. 4.
79. *The Age of Exploration.* Self-Pac® of Basic Education (#104), rev. 1997 (n.p.: Reform Publications, 1974), p. 9.
80. *Old World History*, p. 132.
81. Combee, op. cit., p. 205.
82. Ibid.
83. Thompson and Combee, op. cit., p. 169.
84. Combee, p. 202; Thompson and Combee, op. cit., p. 168.
85. *Old World History*, p. 133.
86. Combee, op. cit., p. 180.
87. Ibid., p. 204.
88. Thompson and Combee, op. cit., pp. 200, 212, 250.
89. Fisher, op. cit., p. 282.
90. Keesee and Sidwell, op. cit., p. 71.
91. Combee, op. cit., p. 203.
92. Ibid., p. 179.
93. Thompson and Combee, op. cit., p. 199.
94. Ibid., p. 200.

95. Fisher, op. cit., p. 283.

96. Thompson and Combee, op. cit., p. 244.

97. Fisher, op. cit., p. 297.

98. Keesee and Sidwell, p. 21.

99. Thompson and Combee, op. cit., p. 266.

100. Fisher, op. cit., p. 296.

101. Ibid.

102. Jan Anderson and Laurel Hicks, *Introduction to English Literature*, 2nd ed. (Pensacola, Fla.: A Beka, 1996), p. 103.

103. Ronald A. Horton, *British Literature for Christian Schools, Teacher's Edition* (Greenville, S.C.: Bob Jones University Press, 1997), p. 153.

104. Ibid. Ironically, Bob Jones' newsletter for home-schooling families, who also use the texts described in this book, identifies "gratuitousness" as one of three reasons that Christians should object to certain literary works. The newsletter asks whether "the representation of evil [is] purposeful or . . . present[ed] for its own sake." "A Biblical Approach to Objective Elements in Literature," *Home School Helper* (October 2002): 6. The other two reasons are "explicitness" ("Is the representation of evil, if purposeful, present in an acceptable degree?") and "moral tone" ("Is evil made to appear both dangerous and repulsive?").

105. *Old World History*, pp. 133, 150.

106. Combee, op. cit., p. 221; Thompson and Combee, p. 258. Emphasis in Combee's seventh-grade text.

107. Combee, op. cit., p. 250.

108. *Old World History*, p. 142.

109. Combee, op. cit., p. 328.

110. Ibid.

111. Ibid.; Thompson and Combee, op. cit., p. 275.

112. Thompson and Combee, op. cit., pp. 266, 268.

113. Ibid., p. 206.

114. Ibid., p. 300.

115. Ibid., p. 106.

116. Keesee and Sidwell, op. cit., p. 8.

117. Ibid.

118. *The Making of Modern Europe.* Self-Pac® of Basic Education (#105). (n.p.: Reform Publications, 1974), p. 4.

119. *Modern Europe*, p. 5.
120. Ibid., p. 5.
121. Ibid., p. 10.
122. Thompson and Combee, op. cit., p. 166.
123. Fisher, op. cit., p. 213.
124. Ibid.
125. Thompson and Combee, op. cit., p. 198.
126. Fisher, op. cit., p. 236.
127. Ibid.
128. *Old World History*, p. 142.
129. Combee, op. cit., p. 242; Thompson and Combee, op. cit., p. 222.
130. Grussendorf, Lowman, and Ashbaugh, op. cit., p. 13.
131. *Age of Exploration*, pp. 3, 6; *American Origins: The Age of Discovery and Explorations.* Self-Pac® of Basic Education (#109), rev. 1995 (n.p.: Reform Publications, 1974), pp. 6, 10.
132. *Age of Exploration*, p. 11.
133. Ibid., pp. 8-9.
134. Ibid.; *American Origins*, pp. 12-13.
135. *Age of Exploration*, p. 9; *American Origins*, p. 13.
136. Thompson and Combee, op. cit., p. 244.
137. Grussendorf, Lowman, and Ashbaugh, op. cit., pp. 16, 17.
138. Thompson and Combee, op. cit., p. 236.
139. Lowman, Thompson, and Grussendorf, op. cit., pp. 15-16.
140. Fisher, op. cit., p. 309.
141. Ibid., p. 318.
142. Keesee and Sidwell, op. cit., p. 71.
143. Ibid., p. 10.
144. *Early Middle Ages*, p. 29.
145. *Age of Exploration*, p. 29; *American Origins*, p. 26.
146. *Approaching the Twenty-First Century.* Self-Pac® of Basic Education (#108), rev. 1997 (n.p.: Reform Publications, 1996), p. 14.
147. *Old World History*, p. 255.
148. Ibid.
149. *Social Studies.* Self-Pac® of Basic Education (#107), rev. 1997 (n.p.: Reform Publications, 1974.), p. 24.
150. *Approaching the Twenty-First Century*, pp. 25-26.
151. See John Higham, *Strangers in the Land: Patterns of American Nativisim, 1860-1925* (New Brunswick, N.J.: Rutgers University

Press, 1992); Dale T. Knoebel, *America for the Americans: The Nativist Movement in the United States* (New York: Simon and Schuster Macmillan, 1996); Chip Berlot and Matthew N. Lyons, *Right-Wing Populism in America: Too Close for Comfort* (New York: Guildford Press, 2000), pp. 46-52, 102, 131-32.

152. "Sadly, today's Evangelicalism is indeed in the business of turfing the road of Roman Catholicism to make it smooth for those traveling thereon to Hell. . . . Evangelical warriors of a bygone age did not fail to label Rome that 'Mother of Harlots,' and would have considered it unthinkable to have fellowship with Romanism." David C. Cloud, *Fundamentalism, Modernism, and New-Evangelicalism, Part II*, online at http://www.camano.net/~dcloud/fbns/fundamen2.htm, cited 21 May 2001. Michael Scheifler's Bible Light Home Page, *Pagan Sun Worship and Catholicism: The Monstrance and the Wafer God,* online at http://www.aloha.net/~mikesch/monstr.htm, cited 21 May 2001. Other documents available on Scheifler's website include *Antichrist, 666, and the Harlot Church, Babylon the Great Is Fallen,* and *Catholicism's Graven Images*. Material available from Chick Publications include: *Are Roman Catholics Christians?* (Ontario, Cal.: Chick Publications, 1985), available at http://www.chick.com/reading/tracts/0071/0071_01.asp (cited 21 May 2001); "Last Rites: When This Catholic Dies, He Learns That His Church Couldn't Save Him" (Ontario, Cal.: Chick Publications, n.d.), available at http://www.chick.com/catalog/tractlist.asp (cited 21 May 2001); and *Why Is Mary Crying? Devotion to Mary Doesn't Please Her. It Breaks Her Heart* (Ontario, Cal.: Chick Publications, 1987), available at http://www.chick.com/reading/tracts/0040/0040 01.asp (cited 21 May 2001).

153. *Faith-Based Funding Backed, but Church-State Doubts Abound* [database online] (Washington, D.C.: Pew Research Center for People & the Press, n.d.), available at http://www.people-press.org/relOlsec2.htm (cited 21 May 2001). To be sure, the respondents rated a variety of other religions unfavorably. Indeed, 16% of the respondents gave an unfavorable or very unfavorable rating to evangelical Christians. But interestingly, while the unfavorable/very unfavorable rating of evangelical Christians

dropped by 1% from September 2000 to March 2001, that of Catholics went up 4%. In fact, evangelical Christians were the only religious group whose ratings declined. Unfavorable/very unfavorable ratings rose 3% and 2% for Muslims and Jews, respectively.

154. Steven Lubet, "The Ten Commandments in Alabama," *Constitutional Commentary* (Fall 1998): 471-78.

155. Ibid., p. 476, quoting Joseph Lewis, *The Ten Commandments* (n.p.: Freethought Press Association, 1946), p. 26.

156. Ibid., quoting Lewis, pp. 26, 28-29.

157. Amy Gutmann, *Democratic Education* (Princeton, N.J.: Princeton University Press, 1987), pp. 29-30.

158. Ibid., p. 31.

159. Ibid., pp. 31-32.

CHAPTER FIVE

"From Cannibals to Christians": Teaching About Non-Western Religions[1]

The authors repeatedly denigrate faiths that are not part of the conservative Protestant tradition. As we saw in Chapter Four, Roman Catholicism is disparaged both explicitly and implicitly. This treatment also extends to discussions of non-Western religions. Gaddy, Hall, and Marzano identify the theological roots that underlie the texts' animus toward non-Western religions. Because truth can only be found in "God's infallible, literal Word revealed in the Bible, *religious* tolerance toward others with different values and different world views must be rejected."[2] Junior high and high school students using A Beka textbooks are told, "The desire to return minority peoples to their tribal roots and religions, a pre-Christian status, is called *multiculturalism*. Some have seen multiculturalism as a new form of segregation that will keep minority groups from becoming part of American culture."[3]

Frequently, criticisms of other religions and Christian denominations revolve around the issue of salvation by faith alone versus salvation by good works; indeed, this was and remains one of the primary differences between Roman Catholicism and Protestantism (even though using the term "salvation" in reference to such non-Western "religions" as Confucianism might seem a bit odd). "Of the different faiths mentioned above [Judaism, Christianity, Islam, Hinduism, Buddhism, Confucianism, Shintoism, and Taoism], all but one require some kind of religious performance or activity to obtain salvation. Only Christianity requires simple faith rather than good works. Only in Christianity is salvation provided through a Person rather than through good works."[4]

A recurring theme is that lack of material progress in various Third World countries and among indigenous peoples can be attributed to their religious beliefs. Failure to follow Western ways, particularly Christianity, leads to cultures that are backward and in some instances causes the people to fall prey to despotic rulers.

The final characteristic that textbooks and materials from all three publishers share when discussing any non-Western religion is a tremendous emphasis on conservative Protestant missionary activity. Coverage of non-Western religions may be sparse or scattered, but approving passages about individual missionaries and Christian converts and the need for both historical and contemporary evangelism abound. This is especially noticeable in Bob Jones' sixth-grade social studies book, A Beka's fifth-grade social studies book, and School of Tomorrow/Accelerated Christian Education materials for fourth-grade social studies.[5] For example, fifth-graders read that "the great pioneer missionary *William Carey* and the missionaries who came after him did much to change the religious practices and the evil worship forms by spreading the gospel in India."[6] In some cases students are exhorted to engage in missionary work as an adult vocation — frequently in countries where "pagan" religions dominate and occasionally in countries where Roman Catholicism is the dominant faith or where the authors perceive a lack of commitment to Protestantism. In the School of Tomorrow/Accelerated Christian Education fourth-grade world geography (world cultures) booklets, each country is approached from the viewpoint of a Christian missionary, either by the device of having a missionary speak to the student body of a fictional Christian school or by a fictionalized account of a contemporary missionary family.[7] In fact, more coverage is given to these accounts and to information about evangelism than to the culture and geography of countries that are the ostensible subjects of the booklets.[8]

Traditional African Religions

In general, A Beka's history textbooks emphasize Africa's need for Christian evangelism.[9] In addition to derogatory comments about the religious beliefs of non-Christian Africans, the textbooks assert that their religious beliefs have been the major cause of the continent's lack of cultural and material progress and political instability and repression. Students reading these highly Eurocentric texts would infer that African culture was inferior to that of white Europeans.[10]

In A Beka's fifth-grade text, students read that traditional African religions were "false religious beliefs [that] spread to the rest of Africa" from the Egyptian descendants of the biblical Ham.[11] Speaking of northern Africa, the author opines that "unfortunately, the descendants of [the biblical] Phut followed a false, pagan religion."[12] Much of the explicit and implicit negative stereotyping of traditional African religions occurs in the two large, highlighted, and illustrated text boxes in the chapter.[13] These text boxes introduce students to a Christian convert, "Khama: A Great African Chief," and a Scottish missionary, "Mary Slessor: Queen of the Cannibals." Although Khama was the son of a "cruel" chief "who was a witch doctor with many wives and who put his own brother to death," he was successful in ruling his people as a Christian in spite of the fact that the "land . . . was ruled by witchcraft" and the people drank their traditional corn beer which made them "lazy and wicked."[14] As a Christian ruler, "he put an end to witchcraft and other wicked practices," including polygamy.[15] While discussing the work of Scottish missionary Mary Slessor, the text uses the term "savage" on three separate occasions.[16] The religious practices of the people Slessor sought to convert are described in pejorative terms:

> When a man died, many of his servants and relatives were killed so the dead man would not have to be alone in his "new life." Because twin babies were thought to be a sign of evil, they were killed. The witch doctors used many evil and cruel practices. Some of the people were cannibals.[17]

Oppressive governments and Communism are ascribed to the influence of traditional African religions. "In countries where the people are still held in fear by witchcraft and spirit worship, [postcolonial] self-government soon turned into dictatorship."[18] The seventh-grade text describes the people of Africa, "the Dark Continent," as "bow[ing] down to wood and stone" and living in "spiritual darkness."[19] Describing and praising the work of David Livingstone allows Combee to include the following statement: "Livingstone believed Africa needed three things: *Christianity*, to end paganism and superstition; commerce to end the slave trade; and civilization, to end the despicable tyranny and oppression on every hand in the 'Dark Continent'."[20] Although neither the junior high nor high school texts posit traditional African religions as a direct cause of Communism, the high school text ascribes southern Africa's failure to progress in a material sense to the absence of Christianity:

> For over a thousand years, there was no clear Christian witness in the vast heartland of Africa; the fear, idolatry, superstition, and witchcraft associated with *animism* (the belief that natural objects and forces are inhabited by mostly malignant spirits) prevented most Africans from learning how to use nature for man's benefit and thus develop a high culture like that of the other African empires.[21]

Praise of missionary activities allows authors to contrast with "inferior" indigenous religions. "Above all else, the missionaries led countless Africans to Christ, discipled them in the Word of God, and thus delivered them from the fear, superstition, and bondage of their native religions."[22] In contemporary Africa, "about 75 percent of the people are in the grips of animistic African religions, and many others are bound by the teachings of Islam."[23] Bob Jones' sixth-grade history text presents traditional African religions in less judgmental fashion but stresses the need for contemporary evangelism. For example, animism is defined as "the belief that objects in nature (trees, mountains, animals, rivers, etc.) have spirits that can bring good or harm to people."[24] Describing the religious practices of the majority of African people, the book states that "many Africans continue to believe that they must keep these spirits happy" and that many Africans "make idols that represent the spirits, wear charms to keep evil away, and offer sacrifices of animals and food."[25] However, Bob Jones's seventh-grade text takes a stronger stance regarding the spiritual error of traditional African religions:

> This religion, like all false religions, is based on works and cannot give blessing or salvation (Ephesians 2:8-9). The strong influence of magic and demonism on African religion made much of African life unhappy and savage. Satan's strong hold on these people kept them worshiping him rather than the true God.[26]

Teachers are advised to "emphasize that African religion was one of superstition and demonism. This kind of religion is growing today in the West, and Christian students must be prepared to stand against it. Satanism is especially prevalent in contemporary music."[27]

Like the A Beka textbooks, the Bob Jones textbooks contrast Christianity with traditional African religions, which are discussed in negative terms. For example, the junior high text declares that Christian missionaries induced many Africans to "leave their heathen worship of idols and evil spirits."[28] Discussing sub-Saharan Africa before the Age of Exploration, the high school text merely states that "most Africans remained in spiritual darkness apart from the light and truth of God's word" (parenthetical material omitted); however, as with the A Beka texts, the description of Mary Slessor's work includes explicitly negative comments about African religion and culture.[29] "Among the many heathen practices which she found among the people, the most appalling was the custom of killing newborn twins."[30] "[Slessor] was responsible for establishing law and order among the wild and savage people."[31] None of Bob Jones' textbooks state or imply that traditional African religions led to lack of progress or contemporary political violence or repression.

Like the A Beka and Bob Jones textbooks discussed above, School of Tomorrow/Accelerated Christian Education materials emphasize the evangelization of the indigenous peoples of Africa and use the term "pagan."[32] Very little is said about the nature of traditional African religions, though factual acknowledgments are made of the religious composition of various countries in the world geography materials. There seem to be only two discussions of traditional African religions. The first describes animism in neutral terms; the second is slightly more pejorative: "When British explorers first began venturing into Africa, they called it the 'dark continent.' Most African tribes believed in the religion of animism. As animists, they believed that all things possessed a soul and also believed in evil spirits and witch doctors."[33]

Asian Religions

Like African religions, Asian religions are described as "pagan." "For centuries the multitudes of people in Asia have been in the grasp of pagan religions."[34] "The [Chinese] Boxers detested Christianity for undermining their pagan beliefs."[35] Similar language, including the phrase, "The hatred of these rebels was directed . . . most particularly perhaps against Christianity, because it undermined their pagan beliefs," is found in the high school text.[36] Even as Roman Catholicism is portrayed as holding Europeans in ignorance of God's true word, Asian religions are accused of holding their adherents in sin. "Hinduism, Buddhism, Islam, and many variations of these bound the people [of India] in their sin."[37] "The strong power of Confucianism, Taoism, Buddhism, and ancestor worship bound many Chinese in their sins."[38]

A fourth-grade School of Tomorrow/Accelerated Christian Education booklet shows how a statement making an implication about sin in Asian cultures is interwoven with a faith statement and culminates with a first-person assertion of belief. "It is important for people to have freedom from sin. Jesus can give the Chinese people freedom from their sin. Someday, when we are all in heaven, we will worship God together with the Chinese people."[39] Several texts purport to show that Chinese ideographs reveal a knowledge of biblical events, especially the Flood, and that Asian peoples lost or abandoned biblical truth in favor of false religions.[40] As with African religions, the texts sometimes ascribe lack of material progress or failure to develop democratic forms of government to the religions of a region:

> The religions and systems of thought founded in both India and China are of great consequence to Asian progress and freedom. Because there was no distinction between religion and politics, the lack of personal freedom in the pagan religions necessarily had its effect in the government. In India and China, the ways of thinking, mainly Hinduism in India and Confucianism in China, dictated the outcome: tyranny. Whenever men are set up in the place of God, there will be a smothering of freedom and a subsequent rise of tyranny. Thus, in both countries, the people were enslaved to false religions and despotic rulers.[41]

Islam. In A Beka's elementary world history text, fifth-graders read that Islam is "a false religion."[42] Seventh-graders read that, although "over 500 people saw the resurrected Jesus Christ, no one witnessed Mohammed's supposed encounters with the angels" and that "because he rejected Jesus Christ as the Son of God Mohammed could not avoid the trap of humanism."[43] According to A Beka's high school textbook, Mohammed "combined elements of a corrupted and distorted Christianity in a legalistic religion."[44] Mohammed is described as a "self-proclaimed prophet" who founded Islam because he "aspir[ed] to religious and political leadership."[45] Islam itself is "a fanatically anti-Christian faith" that has resisted the efforts of Protestant missionaries.[46] The authors' theological difference with Islam is similar to one of their primary criticisms of Roman Catholicism. Because salvation can be achieved by the activities of human beings (as opposed to salvation by grace alone), it falls short of Christian salvation. "External requirements," such as prayer, fasting, giving alms, and making pilgrimages, "involve no true repentance or miraculous regeneration as does Biblical salvation."[47]

Bob Jones' world history text for sixth-graders emphasizes the need for conversion of non-Christians, that is, non-Protestants.

Thus after a fairly straightforward description of Mohammed and the origins of Islam, students read that "the darkness of Islamic religion keeps the people of Turkey from Jesus Christ as their savior."[48] Bob Jones' world history text for middle school/junior high school students gives a great deal more factual information, some of it positive, about Islam and the contributions of the Islamic world; but students are still taught that Islam is "a false religion" and the prayers of its adherents are "worthless words spoken to a false god."[49] The high school text gives a great deal of positive information about the contributions of Islamic people but also comes close to identifying Islam with Satanic religions: "While Muhammad used many biblical terms in his teaching, he distorted biblical truth. Satan often uses this tactic to deceive people."[50] The implication of this comment is unmistakable and, presumably, would be deeply offensive to Muslims. The students also are told that "Islam reflects those characteristics of false prophecy and teaching."[51] This statement is supported by a quotation from Second Peter, which ends, "And many shall follow their pernicious ways; by reason whom the way of truth be evil spoken of."[52] One classroom activity suggested to teachers is to "read selections from the Koran [and] point out . . . how it distorts biblical truth."[53]

The section of a senior high School of Tomorrow/Accelerated Christian Education booklet that discusses Mohammed is liberally sprinkled with the word "supposed," used as an adjective and verb. One subsection, "Supposed Revelation," contains the following sentence: "He was then supposed to have been visited by Gabriel, one of the chief angels."[54] In another section, the term "supposed" is used twice within one sentence. "Mohammed was supposed to have been visited by Gabriel repeatedly within a short time after the first supposed revelation."[55] The students are invited to "think what might have happened if [Mohammed] had encountered the Christ of the Bible. He did not, however, and turned to believing in the concept of Christ as just another prophet and not as God."[56] Mildly but firmly, the text states that "it is to be regretted that the truth of Christ was not Mohammed's truth."[57] In contrast, the discussion of the tenets of Islam, though extremely brief, is factual and objective.

Hinduism. Perhaps the strongest antipathy for non-Christian religions is evinced in the texts' treatment of Hinduism. The term *pagan* is frequently used to describe the Hindu religion and the beliefs of its adherents.[58] The term *evil* is also used.[59] Displaying a distinct and rather startling ethnocentrism, A Beka's fifth-grade history textbook tells students that "although [their] images are really idols, the Hindus refuse to treat them as such."[60] The text emphasizes what it considers to be the negative effects of Hinduism on India: "The effects of Hinduism have been devastating to India's history."[61] Students are asked, "How did Hinduism contribute to this country's sad fate?"[62] To answer this question, students are encouraged to contrast India with the United States. "If we refused to kill disease-carrying insects, allowed filthy animals to roam around in public places, and refused to eat meat for nourishment, do you think we would be as prosperous as we are?"[63] Surprisingly, the antipathy of the elementary school text is muted in A Beka's seventh-grade text. These textbooks may have different authors; the author of the fifth-grade text is not identified. The seventh-grade text describes Hinduism as one of several "pagan religions [that] hindered progress" because, in the case of Hinduism, the caste system resulted in a lack of education for many Indians.[64] Sounding very much like the colonialists of the 18th and 19th centuries, Combee states:

> As a result, the Indian people generally became patient, docile, peaceable, resigned, and polite. They developed none of that ambition which makes men energetic in character and effective in life. They learned little of that self-reliance and sense of personal responsibility that are necessary to the performance of duty.[65]

This statement is followed by a quote from an unidentified scholar arguing that the Hindus are "incapable of writing history

[because] all that happens is dissipated in their minds into confused dreams. What we call historical truth and veracity — intel-
ligent, thoughtful comprehension of events, and fidelity in repre-
senting them — nothing of this sort can be looked for among the
Hindus."[66] Although a good deal less judgmental, A Beka's high
school textbook continues to attribute India's lack of progress to
Hinduism. "The superstition of India's religions is a major cause
of that nation's abject poverty, economic backwardness, and cultural stagnation."[67] Returning to this theme a few pages later, the
authors tie religion and politics together: "Hindu superstition and
socialist ideology continue to hinder India's progress as a
nation."[68]

Bob Jones' sixth-grade text is moderate in tone when compared with A Beka's corresponding elementary text. After an
explanation of how belief in reincarnation has affected Indian
life, the text informs students that "Hindus hold to a false idea of
reincarnation without realizing that the new birth they truly need
is a spiritual birth."[69] Seventh-graders are told that "even those
who strictly followed their Hinduism were simply following a
false religion created by man."[70] In the high school text,
Hinduism, together with Buddhism, is identified merely as a
"pagan religion" whose adherents "fail to realize that even a large
number of good works cannot erase the fact of sin."[71] The School
of Tomorrow/Accelerated Christian Education 10th-grade world
history booklet that includes sections about India and Hinduism
devotes 28 lines to the tenets of Hinduism, of which six lines are
a series of Christian faith statements, for example, "Have you
trusted in Christ as your Savior?"[72] In this section students read
that "[Hinduism] has beliefs and practices of almost any kind"
and that one of the main tenets of Hinduism is that "the world is
evil, and life is all misery."[73] These six lines describing Hinduism
are followed by a faith statement and Bible quotation in which
Hinduism is unfavorably contrasted with Christianity over the
issue of salvation by works versus salvation by grace alone:

> The teachings of Hinduism make the people try to work
> their way to Heaven and are not in agreement with Paul that

salvation is by grace (unearned favor), and men are to merit it: "For by grace are ye saved through faith; and that not of yourselves: it is the gift of God. Not of works, lest any man should boast (Ephesians 2:8-9)."[74]

A ninth-grade world geography (world cultures) booklet gives more extensive coverage. Following a factual discussion of the tenets of Hinduism, the text concludes with a mildly derisive comment concerning reincarnation and incorporates a Christian belief statement:

> Hindus revere all forms of life, because a cow may be one's grandmother in her next life. Obviously, this belief is contrary to the teaching of Scripture, which tells us that our soul, the *essence* of our personality, will spend all eternity either in Heaven with God or separated from God in Hell.[75]

A highlighted text box points out the negative effects, albeit somewhat more politely than the fifth-grade A Beka text, of the Hindu belief in reincarnation: "Cattle and other animals are allowed to roam freely. You can imagine the traffic jams this causes. In addition, the animals cause unsanitary and unhealthy conditions."[76]

Buddhism. Like Islam but unlike Hinduism, Buddhism traces its origins to a particular individual; and Buddha, like Mohammed, is denigrated in Christian school texts. Fifth-graders reading A Beka's history textbook learn that Buddha's search for enlightenment involved "leav[ing] his wife and newborn son" and engaging in unsuccessful "self-torture."[77] The students are reminded that "we serve a living Savior, not a dead teacher."[78] Because it replaced the religion of ancient China that was monotheistic, Buddhism is labeled a "false religion."[79]

For sixth-graders using Bob Jones' *Heritage Studies for Christian Schools* series, each mention of Buddhism is accompanied by a brief passage comparing Buddhism's deficiencies with the true religion of Christianity. For example, students read that "although these [Burmese] Buddhists are sincerely trying to live a good life and do good deeds, they will never receive the peace they seek. . . . These people need to know the Savior."[80] This linkage continues in the junior and senior high school textbooks. Fisher prompts teachers to "be sure to use John 1:1-14 to show the futility of Buddha's search."[81] Both Buddhism and Hinduism are labeled as "pagan religions."[82]

The School of Tomorrow/Accelerated Christian Education materials describe Buddha in terms that are markedly different from its coverage of Mohammed. The text does not interject any value statements or prejudicial language. In discussing Buddhism itself, the emphasis is on telling students how Christianity and Buddhism differ, though the statements are not ones that would be used in public school materials that contrast the two religions to teach comparative religion. Buddhism's nirvana is described as "a type of heaven," and students read that "it is very important to note that Buddha's nirvana was in direct contrast with what the Bible teaches about heaven."[83] Later the text states: "Hinayana Buddhism has retained Buddha's belief in a lifeless heaven where people would have no knowledge of being alive. Jesus Christ directly opposed this belief in John 3:15-17 and many other passages."[84]

Confucianism. Even as the disapproval of Buddhism is not as vehement as that directed at Hinduism, negative comments about Confucianism are even more muted. A Beka's fifth-grade text acknowledges that the philosophy ("many people consider his teachings to be a religion") has "many good points" but some "weaknesses."[85] The author reminds students that "salvation comes only [through the] One Who knew no sin at all, the Lord Jesus Christ."[86] The junior high school text makes a similar comment regarding Confucianism's primary deficiency — that it is not Christian — accompanied by a brief statement of faith. The high school text omits the faith statement.

Bob Jones's sixth-grade text, after describing Confucius and mentioning Chinese Buddhism, simply states that the Chinese "had not found the One they needed to know," includes a quotation from Proverbs, and laments that Christian missionaries had not been very successful in China. In the high school text, students read merely that "the major defect of Confucius's teaching was his neglect of the most important relationship of all — man and God."[87] A statement of Christian faith leading into a scriptural quotation follows.

School of Tomorrow/Accelerated Christian Education materials have relatively little to say about Chinese religions or philosophies and have substantially fewer and less negative comments than either A Beka or Bob Jones textbooks. A mere assertion, combined with a first-person faith statement, that these religious philosophies are in error constitutes the only critical commentary: "After these philosophers died, some of their followers began to worship them. The Bible says we are to worship God only; therefore, we know it was wrong for the Chinese people to worship these dead philosophers as ancestors."[88]

Taoism. Taoism is not mentioned in A Beka's elementary text, but the junior and senior high textbooks give it a treatment almost as mild as that accorded Confucianism. Junior high school students read that "desperate for assurance of future life, some Taoists groups have in vain sought immortality by means special diets, meditation, and magic."[89] Although the following passages do not specifically mention Taoism, it is not unreasonable to assume the author intended to show that its tenets were a major contributor to China's lack of scientific progress, or at least to its failure to take "progressive measures . . . founded on scientific principles" because their "unscientific approach to nature is the product of Asiatic paganism."[90] Asians put themselves rather than God at the center of their relationship to the natural world. "Man . . . worship[s] himself . . . rather than the Creator" and "relinquishes his individuality."[91]

> Paradoxically . . . *this humanistic view of nature actually stifles man's achievement* because he is overly awed by nature and does not strive to subdue it as Scripture commands. Thus, instead of conquering and mastering nature,

he becomes a slave to its tyranny. Since the main motive of science is mastery of nature, the Asians were left without the motivating force for more substantial, consequential levels of cultural and economic activity.[92]

Bob Jones' history textbooks display a somewhat more judgmental attitude when discussing Taoism but do not link it to other Asian religions. For seventh-graders the philosophy's passivism and emphasis on living in harmony with nature are contrasted with cultures whose religions are rooted in the Judeo-Christian tradition: "This religion contradicts God's commandment to subdue the earth (Genesis 1: 28) and to evangelize the world (Matthew 28: 19-20)."[93] Taken literally, this is a somewhat difficult statement because it faults Taoists for the their failure to evangelize on behalf of a religion that the textbook authors obviously regard as false and evil: "These confused people had been blinded by the god of this world, the devil."[94] High school students read that "Taoism favors a past existence and attempts to free man from responsibility" and that "Taoists reject external authority and stress noninvolvement in society."[95]

Shintoism. A Beka's seventh-grade text tells students that "nature has complete mastery over followers of Shintoism" and its adherents "enshrine man and natural objects alike as gods."[96] Writing for high school students, A Beka authors, Thompson and Combee, describe Shintoism in one sentence while devoting a great deal of attention to Protestant evangelism in Japan, including the work of Jonathan Goble, "the first Baptist missionary to Japan," and Neesima, "Japan's most famous Christian."[97]

Bob Jones' sixth-grade text begins its chapter on Japan with the fictional story of a young Japanese girl who attends a Bible club with a Western friend. Although the Japanese family objects, the girl's mother gives permission. This literary device allows the chapter on Japan to begin with a statement of Christian beliefs ("Because we have all sinned, we need Jesus to save us from our sins"), a Bible story ("Zacchaeus trusted in Jesus, and he was saved. . . . All of us, like Zacchaeus, need to realize we are sinners"), and a portrayal of the presumably Protestant missionaries as warm and kindly persons.[98] Speaking of both Buddhism and Shintoism, the text explains that "despite all their rituals, prayers, and traditions, most of the Japanese people are lost in sin [and] still need the Saviour."[99] For seventh-graders, followers of Shintoism are compared with the Pharisees of the Bible: "They are very similar to the Jewish Pharisees whom Jesus condemned for putting outward cleanliness above inward purity."[100] High school students are given an objective description of Shintoism that concludes: "In modern times the Japanese government made Shintoism into a national cult, which required belief in the ancient myths, encouraged patriotism, and maintained the prestige of the Emperor."[101]

Religions of Oceania and the Pacific Islands

A Beka's fifth-grade text includes two pictures of Maoris standing with some carved poles. The caption asks, "What about their surroundings tells you that some of the people still have ancient pagan beliefs?"[102] The junior and senior high school texts use identical language to convey the benefits of both evangelism and colonialism.[103] "The countries of the Empire greatly profited from Britain as well, for she shared two most important gifts with them: her Christian faith and her representative form of government."[104] Speaking of the colonization of Australia, the authors of both texts point out that "missionaries were sent to the Aborigines, the original inhabitants of the land. As Biblical standards of morality were established and under Britain's watchful eye, Australian society grew more stable" (parenthetical phonetic spelling omitted).[105] This passage suggests that Aboriginal society and culture were unstable. Eighth-graders learn that the native Hawaiians, as discovered by Captain Cook, were "a heathen people devoted to superstition, human sacrifice, and idol worship."[106] High school students reading A Beka's American history text learn that "the main religious bodies [of the Philippines] were Catholics, Moslems, and pagans."[107]

The need for contemporary evangelism is stressed in Bob Jones' sixth-grade history and geography text. Aborigines "have their traditional religious ceremonies and practices that involve nature worship [but] need to learn of the salvation that God has provided through Jesus Christ."[108] Speaking of the Pacific Islanders, the text opines, "Although most Samoans and Pacific Islanders claim to be 'Christians,' belief in spirits and other native superstitions continue."[109] "Early missionaries brought Christianity to [Papua New Guinea], and now most people claim to be Christian [but] most continue, however, to believe in spirits and to practice sorcery."[110] A "spirit house" on the island is described as having "ugly masks and carved figures."[111] In Bob Jones' high school text, almost as much coverage is given to missionary efforts in Australia and New Zealand as is given to the general discussion of the two nations. In conjunction with information about the life of Samuel Marsden, "an evangelical Anglican," students read that "in the early nineteenth century, many people believed that the heathen could not be won until they were civilized."[112]

Native American Religions

Much of the coverage of Native Americans centers on the violence between Native Americans and colonists and settlers, emphasizing Native American attacks on whites. Both the textbooks and School of Tomorrow/Accelerated Christian Education materials also stress Native Americans' need for and benefit from conversion to Christianity, though the A Beka and Bob Jones materials de-emphasize the negative effects of European and white American influence. "God's word is far more valuable than anything else Europeans brought to America. . . . Influenced by the Bible, Indians, like other Americans would later have the opportunity to enjoy freedom and liberty and play a role in building the country."[113] In a remarkable display of cultural insensitivity, the authors of A Beka's junior high school American history book tell students that "God used the Trail of Tears to bring many

Indians to Christ."[114] The authors go on to assert that "eventually, the benefits of Christian civilization — education, high moral standards, medical science, modern agricultural technology and commerce — would eliminate tribal warfare and famine and make the Indian population larger and healthier than ever before."[115] Much of the coverage of Native Americans is devoted to approving accounts of white missionaries and Christian converts.

A Beka's fourth-grade American history textbook begins relatively benignly: "Indians were isolated from the gospel and had never seen the Scriptures. Each tribe made its own religion. Some worshiped idols; some worshiped the sun and the moon."[116] Violence between the Plains tribes and the settlers is explained in terms of the killing of the buffalo, promises broken by "white men," "cruelty on both sides," and the "many false religions [of Native Americans that] had made it hard for the Indians and white men to get along."[117] Both A Beka's junior and senior high school American history texts state that it is likely the first Americans migrated to North America after Noah's flood. For example: "The first people to come to the New World were probably hunters following the trail of the animals that had begun to multiply and spread out over the earth after the Flood."[118] This statement segues into the assertion that "the early American Indians, like most other people, had forsaken the things that their ancestors knew about God."[119] In particular, the authors note, "their stories about the Creation and the Flood were not accurate."[120] The high school text substitutes, "Rather than worshiping the Creator, they worshiped creation, particularly things they could not understand such as thunder, wind, fire, and the sun."[121] For the authors, the failure of Native Americans to make European style material progress was a result of their traditional tribal religions: "Because superstition kept the Indians from working together to develop the land in which they lived, America would remain a wilderness until the Europeans arrived."[122] The intervening material related to Native Americans focuses on the violence between white colonists and settlers, especially Native American attacks on white settlers and the desirable and successful evangelization of the Native American population. A short paragraph, consisting of three sentences on the subject of contemporary Native American life, ends, "Missionary activities continue on many Indian reservations."[123] Although Bob Jones' history textbooks occasionally mention the need for the evangelization and conversion of Native Americans, they do not discuss the nature of their religion.

In contrast to the A Beka and Bob Jones textbooks, School of Tomorrow/Accelerated Christian Education booklets frequently include statements that are critical of how white colonists and settlers treated Native Americans and some statements that purport, albeit it somewhat clumsily at times, to include a Native American perspective. In some instances the criticism of whites contains a faith statement. Eleventh-graders read that "in many cases man's greedy, sinful nature caused him to mistreat the native Americans who were here before him and ravage the very land that God had given him."[124] The authors, like those of A Beka's fourth-grade American history textbook, imply the idea that the coexistence of Christians and non-Christians in the nation is not a desirable state of affairs: "Bloody conflicts with the Indians" is one result of America's "mixed saved-unsaved population" in that "America has been populated with the lost and saved alike."[125]

As in the A Beka and Bob Jones materials, great emphasis is placed on missionary activities. As with Grussendorf, Lowman, and Ashbaugh seeing providentialism in the Trail of Tears, another of ACE's 11th-grade American history booklets states, "[Roger] Williams' exile may not have seemed like a blessing at first, but God used it to bring the Gospel of Jesus Christ to the Indians."[126] Evangelism is portrayed in a positive light and identified as the cause of events that could be ascribed to other causes. For example, an 11th-grade booklet finds that "early missionary efforts were basic causal factors in producing the climate out of which grew the Five Civilized Tribes of the Southeast."[127] Discussions of missionary activity sometimes include pejorative comments about Native Americans. For example, "[John] Elliot traveled far and wide preaching the Gospel to the lost, copper-skinned North Americans."[128] *The Age of Exploration* describes the early French influence on Native Americans: "They failed to bring Christianity and civilization to the Indians, but became savages themselves."[129]

Very little information about the actual nature of Native American religions is included in School of Tomorrow/Accelerated Christian Education materials; but when it occurs, the discussion frequently includes pejorative comments, statements of faith, or both. After briefly retelling a Hopi legend about the migration of their ancestors to the Americas, a senior high school American history booklet uses the present tense to make the following point in a discussion of contemporary Hopis. "Although this was a heathen legend, it bears the seed of a basic moral lesson. Even these *primitive pagans* recognize the difference between good and evil and the need for living decent lives. How much more should we as Christians order our lives after the moral precepts of Almighty God" (emphasis added).[130] An eighth-grade geography booklet also retells this myth with similar comments: "Pagan Indians recognized in an imperfect way, God is in charge of every event in human history including the coming of the first Americans to the Americas."[131] Perhaps the harshest statement in School of Tomorrow/Accelerated Christian Education materials regarding Native American religions occurs in this booklet: "We must . . . remember that the Indians were worshipers of demons and false gods and practiced many un-Godly acts."[132]

Concluding Comments

As I commented in Chapter Two, the vast amount of the material in these textbooks and the School of Tomorrow/Accelerated Christian Education booklets would be unobjectionable to anyone. Map studies, discussions of Revolutionary War battles, information about the kings and queens of England, facts about the invention of the cotton gin, and descriptions of the geographical features of Turkey would raise no questions about their propriety as schoolbooks for young people. On the other hand, many statements related to non-Western religions raise serious issues that should be part of the public debate over the use of public funding for sectarian education and the use of these materials for home schooling. These issues can be encompassed by a series of questions: What might be the result if students who used such materials as a significant part of their schooling were to seek to serve the United States in its diplomatic corps? Would adults who had been taught in schools using these textbooks make good decisions on foreign policy if they were to become members of Congress? Could voters whose education background included substantial exposure to such materials make reasoned choices about the policies of their elected representatives? How much respect for the rights of members of minority religions could ordinary citizens, elected representatives, and government employees, including judges, have if their education background included a school curriculum based on these textbooks? Religious-political conservatives have displayed and continue to display strong animus toward non-Western religious traditions.[133] In 1999 Representative Bob Barr of Georgia objected to the inclusion of Wiccans among groups permitted to conduct religious ceremonies on military bases, and the Family Research Council objected to the delivery of Congress' opening by a Hindu in the fall of 2000.[134] In the spring of 2001, the conservative organization, Campus Crusade for Christ, distributed a flyer implying that had the people of India been Christian instead of Hindu and Muslim, they might have been spared the devastation of a "massive cyclone and tidal wave."[135]

When the public funding of sectarian education is the issue under consideration, a further question arises: Is it fair to use the coercive power of the state to collect tax revenues which are in turn used to support education institutions that malign the religion of the taxpayer? It is one thing to say, "This is what I believe." It is something else to say, "Your religion is in error."

And it is surely far removed from the spirit of religious tolerance, however imperfectly applied in our nation, to make statements that encourage American children to despise the religions of their fellow citizens. It is this point that Ralph Reed, former executive director of the Christian Coalition, makes in relation to public education in his 1994 book, *Politically Incorrect.* Reed writes that even as "African American parents do not want their third-grader learning language that denigrates their race [so too] deeply religiously people do not want their children taught ideas [in public schools] about morality that directly contradict their religious beliefs."[136] It is not unreasonable to suppose that minority faith parents would not want their children "learning language that denigrates their" religion and that Muslims and Hindus, among others, would strongly object to the use of such materials in schools their children attended. Indeed, Reed calls "attacks on religion the equivalent of kidney punches that should be against the rules."[137] Yet shortly after he wrote these words, the Christian Coalition's Contract with the American Family advocated school-choice programs that would include sectarian schools. His statements regarding attacks on religion are wholly inconsistent with his support for school choice unless he was unaware, as I believe many policy makers and activists are, of the nature of the curricula used in a number of Christian schools.

Fundamentally, education concerns not only the right of parents and families to transmit their beliefs and values to their children, but also society's right to educate its future citizens for the collective good. We have the right to insist on education that is benign and that encourages tolerance. Writer Amy Gutmann argues that both toleration and mutual respect are critical to our collective:

> Toleration — an attitude of live and let live entails no positive regard among citizens — is an essential value of American constitutional democracy. Toleration makes peace possible, a precondition for all other democratic accomplishments. But toleration is not enough to create a democratic society with liberty and justice for all, where "all"

includes people of differing religions, ethnicities, color, and
cultures. Absent mutual respect, people discriminate against
each other on the basis of a host of cultural differences.[138]

Gutmann argues that schools should be places in which "students learn to reflect, individually and collectively, on both the
reasonable differences and commonalities that constitute a plu-
ralistic democracy."[139]

In these textbooks there is both an arrogance and a hostility
toward practitioners of non-Western religions that is truly breath-
taking. Would students reading these materials find the differences between themselves and the groups of people discussed in
the chapter "reasonable"? How could they find commonality with
individuals whose most deeply held beliefs are believed to be
inspired by Satan?

If toleration makes peace possible, and if these textbooks not
only fail to foster tolerance but in many instances actively inculcate antipathy toward a number of religious groups, then one
question that must be confronted is whether they come close to a
form of religious hate speech. Scholar Yael Tamir acknowledges
that not all religion is benevolent and asks, "What if religious
teachings have unsettling, even dangerous, social and political
outcomes?"[140] Tamir defines religious hate speech as "religious in
a dual sense: (a) it is delivered by religious leaders who make
repeated references to religious texts [and] (b) it is delivered in
religious institutions and in other religious spaces."[141] And it is
hate speech if it "inflicts injury."[142]

Could one consider the authors of these textbooks to be "religious leaders"? Although they are not, as far as I was able to
ascertain, members of the clergy, a reasonable case can be made
for their being considered religious leaders because they are
authors of religious textbooks. It is entirely likely that students
who read these textbooks would consider their authors to be religious leaders. Certainly, they cite and quote scripture frequently
and make religious statements. When the textbooks are used in
church or religious schools, they are being used in religious institutions and religious spaces, regardless of whether one considers

the school itself a "religious institution or other religious space." That a considerable amount of the material in the A Beka, Bob Jones, and Accelerated Christian Education textbooks is religious speech is beyond doubt, either on a commonsense level or as defined by Tamir. But is it hate speech, language that, intentionally or not, hurts and humiliates or, in the words of Kent Greenawalt, "inflicts injury"?[143] Greenawalt lists several characteristics of objectionable speech that encompass the language used by the authors of these textbooks when they discuss non-Western religions. First, such speech inflicts "psychological hurt for persons who are the object of abuse." Second, its use causes "general offense." Third, such language leads to "long-term destructive effects from attitudes reinforced by abusive remarks."[144] The reader must judge whether Muslims, Hindus, Buddhists, or members of other minority faiths would find that the descriptions of their religions and cultures in these textbooks cause "psychological hurt." This requires a degree of empathy, the ability to imagine oneself in the place of the other. I believe a reasonable person would find the characterizations of non-Western religions to be "generally offensive."

The comments about religious minorities found in the textbooks discussed in this chapter and in Chapter Four will have a "long-term destructive effect" because such language encourages religious and cultural intolerance and enmity between groups. Both Tamir and Greenawalt argue for the suppression of such speech, Greenawalt through the imposition of civil penalties.[145] "Hate speech can seriously interfere with equality, restriction of it . . . implements a constitutional value."[146] This is a proposition of dubious constitutionality, as the United States Court of Appeals for the Ninth Circuit found in March 2001 when it held that even threatening speech is not subject to civil penalties.[147] But there is considerable difference between suppressing offensive speech and encouraging it by various funding mechanisms. The Constitution may forbid the government to penalize (by imposing monetary damages) organizations that disseminate material that threatens abortion providers, for example; but it does not oblige the government to provide funds to such organizations. Only if the notion of free speech is stretched to include financial support, as a governmental benefit, can we justify using public funds to support schools that use textbooks that denigrate the religions of millions of Americans.

The old adage, "Be careful what you wish for," applied when Congress voted the Equal Access Act into law, in part because religious-political conservatives wanted Christian students to have the right to form religious clubs in public schools. At the time, some naysayers pointed out that schools would not be able to discriminate against clubs with messages that many would find offensive, say, a Satanist group or the Klu Klux Klan. When the challenge came, it was in the form of gay and lesbian student groups seeking to form clubs. Around the edges of the privatization movement, tiny eddies of disturbance swirl around the seemingly farfetched possibility of public funding for schools run by the Klan, militia groups, and white supremacists. The material described in Chapters Four and Five demonstrates that the problem of funding schools that engage in speech that many, if not most, Americans would find offensive is considerably less remote and hypothetical than those worst-case scenarios.

Notes

1. An article with this title appeared in the *Valdosta* (Georgia) *Daily Times* in December 1998. Although the article, which focused on missionary activity in Papua New Guinea, was not critical of the indigenous peoples of the region, the tone was condescending. The article emphasized how the diet of the people of Papua New Guinea differs from that of Americans by including references to the consumption of snakes (including a picture identified as a "villager carr[ying] a baked snake" (the caption uses the term "baked snake" twice), spiders, bats, and grub worms (a second of the four illustrations shows a boy with a grub worm protruding from his mouth). Repeatedly, the article makes reference to the people of the island killing each other and to their cannibalism. E. R. Butler, "From Cannibals to Christians: Local Man Shares the Lord's Word in Former Land of Cannibalism," *Valdosta Daily Times*, 13 December 1998, p. D1.

2. Barbara. B. Gaddy, T. William Hall, and Robert J. Marzano, *School Wars: Resolving Our Conflicts over Religion and Values* (San Francisco: Jossey-Bass, 1996), p. 145.
3. Kurt A. Grussendorf, Michael R. Lowman, and Brian S. Ashbaugh, *America: Land That I Love, Teacher Edition* (Pensacola, Fla.: A Beka, 1994), p. 511; Michael R. Lowman, George Thompson, and Kurt Grussendorf, *United States History in Christian Perspective: Heritage of Freedom*, 2nd ed. (Pensacola, Fla.: A Beka, 1996), p. 676. Multicultural education can lead children to "experience the particular practices, prayers, chants, and beliefs of religions such as Islam, Hinduism, and Native American shamanism, which can include magic and witchcraft" (Gaddy, Hall, and Marzano, p, 129).
4. *World Geography-10.* Social Studies (#1106), rev. 1998. (n.p.: Accelerated Christian Education, 1994), p. 6.
5. "Today the Jews of Israel and those living in other countries need to learn that they must have Christ's righteousness through faith" *Heritage Studies for Christian Schools 6: Eastern Hemisphere Nations* (Greenville, S.C.: Bob Jones University Press, 1986), p. 174.
6. *Old World History and Geography, Teacher Edition* (Pensacola, Fla.: A Beka, 1991), p. 213.
7. See generally School of Tomorrow/Accelerated Christian Education social studies study packs (booklets) numbers 41 through 48 (on the booklets these are labeled 1041 to 1048; catalog numbers are 8041 through 8048).
8. *India*, Social Studies 1041, rev. 1998 (n.p.: Accelerated Christian Education, 1981); *Africa*, Social Studies 1043, rev. 1998 (n.p.: Accelerated Christian Education, 1981); *China*, Social Studies 1044, rev. 1998 (n.p.: Accelerated Christian Education, 1981); *Burma*, Social Studies 1045, rev. 1998 (n.p.: Accelerated Christian Education, 1981); and *Ecuador*, Social Studies 1046, rev. 1998 (n.p.: Accelerated Christian Education, 1981). Other booklets for this grade level include map studies, missions to 19th century England, and American history and government.
9. The term "Christian" applies only to conservative Protestant evangelism. Missionary activity by other Christian denominations, including Roman Catholic missionary activity, is ignored, given perfunctory coverage, or criticized or ridiculed.

10. Although this chapter focuses on the treatment of religion, several aspects of the textbooks' treatment of Africa in general warrant at least a cursory discussion. First, in keeping with a literal interpretation of the Bible, the African peoples are identified as "descendants of Ham's sons, Mizraim, Phut and Cush [who] migrated to Africa from Babel." George Thompson and Jerry Combee, *World History and Cultures in Christian Perspective* (Pensacola, Fla.: A Beka, 1997), p. 82. See also A Beka's fifth-grade book, *Old World History*, p. 247. Second, A Beka texts use the pejorative phrase, "the Dark Continent." In A Beka's fifth-grade text, this phrase is accompanied by the explanation that not much was known about Africa during its exploration by Europeans. In the junior high and high school texts, this explanation is omitted. Third, the elementary textbook contains a number of gratuitous examples of aspects of African culture that imply that African culture was and remains primitive and violent.

11. *Old World History*, p. 247.

12. Ibid.

13. Ibid., pp. 252-53, 255.

14. Ibid., p. 252.

15. Ibid., pp. 252-53.

16. "Savage warriors," "savage tribe," and "savage land." Ibid., p. 256.

17. Ibid.

18. Ibid., p. 256-57.

19. Jerry H. Combee, *History of the World in Christian Perspective, Teacher Edition*, 3rd ed. (Pensacola, Fla.: A Beka, 1997), pp. 420, 423, 427. No source is given for the quotation "bow down to wood and stone."

20. Ibid., p. 422.

21. Thompson and Combee, op. cit. p. 86.

22. Ibid., p. 89.

23. Ibid., p. 92.

24. *Heritage Studies for Christian Schools 6*, pp. 364, 365.

25. Ibid., p. 365.

26. *World Studies for Christian Schools, Teacher's Edition* (Greenville, S.C.: Bob Jones University Press, 1993), p. 353.

27. Ibid., p. 78T.

28. Ibid., p. 495.

29. David A. Fisher, *World History for Christian Schools, Teacher's Edition* (Greenville, S.C.: Bob Jones University Press, 1994), p. 173.

30. Ibid., p. 490.

31. Ibid., p. 491.

32. "In southern Sudan, most people . . . practice pagan religions." *World Geography-3*, Social Studies (#1099), rev. 1996 (n.p.: Accelerated Christian Education, 1994, p. 16). "The native [South] Africans . . . worshiped pagan gods" (p. 27). In contrast, "most Zambians are Bible believers" (p. 21).

33. *Approaching the Twenty-First Century*, Self-Pac® of Basic Education (#108), rev. 1997 (n.p.: Reform Publications, 1996), p. 57. A different booklet partially undercuts this use of the term "dark continent" ("what they discovered was not a 'dark' continent, but rather a continent of fascinating contrasts"), but here the text implies that places in which animistic religions are practiced are "dark." *World Geography-3*, p. 5.

34. *Old World History*, p. 208.

35. Grussendorf, Lowman, and Ashbaugh, op. cit., p. 363.

36. Lowman, Thompson, and Grussendorf, op. cit., p. 460.

37. *World Studies*, p. 460.

38. Ibid., p. 472.

39. *Social Studies 1044*, p. 32.

40. See Fisher, op. cit., p. 153; Thompson and Combee, op. cit., p. 50; *Social Studies 1044*, p. 27.

41. Combee, op. cit., p. 284.

42. *Old World History*, p. 89.

43. Combee, op. cit., pp. 147, 151.

44. Thompson and Combee, op. cit., p. 34.

45. Ibid., pp. 34-35.

46. Ibid., p. 36.

47. Ibid., p. 35.

48. *Heritage Studies for Christian Schools 6*, p. 186.

49. *World Studies*, pp. 217, 218. The section on "The Islamic World" is introduced by a story of a young Arab boy whose family decides to flee from their village or town because they fear forced conversion to Islam (pp. 209-12).

50. Fisher, op. cit., p. 138.

51. Ibid.

52. Ibid., p. 138, quoting 2 Pet. 1-2.
53. Ibid., p. 139.
54. *Early Middle Ages*, Self-Pac® of Basic Education (#101), rev. 1995 (n.p.: Reform Publications, 1974), p. 17.
55. Ibid., p. 18.
56. Ibid., p. 17.
57. Ibid., p. 18.
58. See, for example, *Old World History*, p. 210.
59. *Old World History*, pp. 213, 214.
60. Ibid., p. 211.
61. The high school text also mentions idols. A discussion of Indian contributions to the world is prefaced by this phrase: "Although India culture was dominated by Hindu idolatry." Thompson and Combee, op. cit., p. 47.
62. *Old World History*, p. 211.
63. Ibid., p. 211.
64. Combee, op. cit., p. 279.
65. Ibid., p. 279.
66. Ibid.
67. Thompson and Combee, op. cit., p. 44.
68. Ibid., p. 47. Presumably it is the nature of the religion and kind of political ideology that are the difficulty. Christianity and capitalism would yield a positive result. See Chapter Two.
69. *Heritage Studies for Christian Schools 6*, p. 199.
70. *World Studies*, p. 207.
71. Fisher, op. cit., pp. 147, 148.
72. *Early Middle Ages*, p. 30. An additional 12 lines in another part of the booklet describe the caste system and briefly mention Hinduism (p. 27).
73. Ibid., p. 30.
74. Ibid. One of the review questions for this section includes the following fill-in-the-blank statement: "We who are Christians believe that _____ died and arose from the dead for us" (p. 31).
75. *World Geography-10*, p. 5.
76. Ibid., p. 21.
77. *Old World History*, p. 212.
78. Ibid., p. 212.
79. Thompson and Combee, op. cit., p. 50.

80. *Heritage Studies for Christian Schools 6*, pp. 222-23.
81. Fisher, op. cit., p. 148.
82. Ibid.
83. *Early Middle Ages*, p. 31.
84. Ibid.
85. *Old World History*, p. 224.
86. Ibid.
87. Fisher, op. cit., p. 154.
88. *Social Studies 1066*, rev. 1998 (n.p.: Accelerated Christian Education, 1982), p. 34.
89. Combee, op. cit., p. 282.
90. Ibid., p. 283.
91. Ibid.
92. Ibid. Note the militaristic tone of this passage resulting, in large part, from the use of words that connote relationships based on inequalities of power: "subdue," "conquer," "master," "slave," and "tyranny."
93. *World Studies*, p. 88.
94. Ibid.
95. Fisher, op. cit., p. 154.
96. Combee, op. cit., pp. 284-85.
97. Thompson and Combee, op. cit., pp. 56-57. A description of Neesima's life occupies a half-page, highlighted text box. The opening of Japan to contact with the West came about, at least in part, because "burdened Christians prayed that God would open Japan to missions [and] God answered those prayers through an action of the U.S. government." Thompson and Combee, p. 56.
98. *Heritage Studies for Christian Schools 6*, pp. 259-66, 265. The missionary family does not disparage the Japanese child's religion, though the Japanese family uses the term "foolish" in reference to Christianity when discussing whether their daughter should accept the invitation to the Bible club (p. 264).
99. Ibid., p. 268.
100. *World Studies*, p. 180.
101. Fisher, op. cit., p. 160.
102. *Old World History*, p. 265.
103. For a discussion of Eurocentrism in right-wing ideology, see Chip Berlot and Matthew N. Lyons, *Right-Wing Populism in*

America: Too Close for Comfort (New York: Guildford Press, 2000), pp. 328-39.

104. Combee, op. cit., p. 429; Thompson and Combee, op. cit., p. 375.

105. Combee, op. cit., p. 429; Thompson and Combee, op. cit., p. 375. Whether the previously discussed transported convicts (who had "settled into a life of idleness, drunkenness, thievery, immorality"), the aborigines, or both groups were in need of "Biblical standards" is ambiguous; nevertheless, the statement does immediately follow one that describes the sending of missionaries to the indigenous peoples of Australia. Combee, p. 429; Thompson and Combee, p. 375.

106. Grussendorf, Lowman, and Ashbaugh, op. cit., p. 223.

107. Lowman, Thompson, and Grussendorf, op. cit., p. 438.

108. *Heritage Studies for Christian Schools 6*, p. 310.

109. Ibid., p. 291.

110. Ibid., p. 297.

111. Ibid., p. 298. This same publisher's junior high school textbook describes the masks used in African religious ceremonies as "often [having] ugly faces with deformed features." *World Studies*, p. 355. This judgmental attitude also is present in discussions of European art. "Artists and writers . . . rejected conventional art forms [and] portrayed a pessimistic and disjointed view of man, his world, and the future." Fisher, op. cit., p. 543. This pessimism is attributed to humanity's turning away from God's comfort (p. 546). Modern art embodies liberal values that reject absolute values. For example, abstract art expresses the artist's "own subjective thoughts and feelings in a chaotic arrangement of shapes and colors." Thompson and Combee, op. cit., p. 454. By contrast, "conservative art" has "won a place in the hearts of most people" because "people can easily relate" to "traditional forms" (p. 455). See Chapter One for additional discussion of these authors' attitudes toward modern art.

112. Fisher, op. cit., p. 278. It is unclear whether the viewpoint expressed in this statement is confined to the nineteenth century. The author does not distance himself or disavow either the sentiment or the term "heathen."

113. *The History of Our United States. Teacher Edition* (Pensacola, Fla.: A Beka, 1998), p. 64. A similar sentiment regarding the

necessity of conversion to be prepared for liberty is made in A Beka's senior high school American history book. Lowman, Thompson, and Grussendorf, op. cit., p. 219. See Chapter Two.

114. Grussendorf, Lowman, and Ashbaugh, op. cit., p. 220. It might be more accurate to say the relative importance placed on the doctrine of providentialism as opposed to cultural sensitivity. The statement concerning the Trail of Tears is reinforced by being included in the chapter review questions.

115. Ibid., p. 254.

116. *History of Our United States*, p. 61.

117. Ibid., p. 227.

118. Grussendorf, Lowman, and Ashbaugh, op. cit., p. 9. This view of the origin of Native Americans is repeated in several Bob Jones textbooks and School of Tomorrow/Accelerated Christian Education materials, for example, "Sometime after the Noachian Flood and the attempt by rebellious men to build the Tower of Babel, numerous Mongoloid peoples from Siberia began migrating to the Americas." *American Origins: The Age of Discovery and Explorations*, Self-Pac® of Basic Education (#109), rev. 1995 (n.p.: Reform Publications, 1974), p. 2. It is consistent with explanations of the historical origins of other ethnic groups given in these texts. See also *Social Studies 1050* (n.p.: Accelerated Christian Education, 1981), p. 10; *Social Studies 1085*, rev. 1998 (n.p.: Accelerated Christian Education, 1990), p. 5; *Age of Reform, 1865-1900*, Self-Pac® of Basic Education (#117), rev. 1996, (n.p.: Reform Publications, 1974), p. 9.

119. Grussendorf, Lowman, and Ashbaugh, op. cit., p. 10.

120. Ibid.

121. Lowman, Thompson, and Grussendorf, op. cit., p. 7.

122. Ibid. Note the similarity to assertions made about African and Asian religions as primary causes of failure to make material progress.

123. Grussendorf, Lowman, and Ashbaugh, op. cit., p. 332.

124. *Westward Expansion*, Self-Pac® of Basic Education (#115), rev. 1995 (n.p.: Reform Publications, 1974), p. 46.

125. Ibid., p. 37.

126. *Colonial Period*, Self-Pac® of Basic Education (#110), rev. 1995 (N.p.: Reform Publications, 1974), p. 23.

127. *Rising Sectionalism*, Self-Pac® of Basic Education (#113) (n.p.: School of Tomorrow, 1974), p. 27.

128. *Colonial Period*, p. 25.

129. *The Age of Exploration*, Self-Pac® of Basic Education (#104), rev. 1997 (n.p.: Reform Publications, 1974), p. 30. This failure is contrasted with the positive influence of the Huguenots, "victims of persecution and repeated atrocities at the hands of French Catholics," who were under the leadership of "the Protestant statesman, Gaspard de Coligny" (p. 30). See Chapter Four.

130. *American Origins*, p. 4.

131. *Social Studies 1085*, p. 5.

132. Ibid., p. 31.

133. Frances R.A. Paterson, *Legally Related Religious Challenges to Public School Materials, Curricula, and Instructional Activities: The "Impressions" Challenges, 1986-1994* (Ann Arbor, Mich.: University Microfilms, 1997), pp. 53-54, 238-41; Constance E. Cumbey, *The Hidden Dangers of the Rainbow: The New Age Movement and Our Coming Age of Barbarism*, rev. ed. (Lafayette, La.: Huntington House, 1983), pp. 168-69; Douglas R. Groothuis, *Unmasking the New Age* (Downers Grove, Ill.: InterVarsity, 1986), p. 140; Texe Marrs, *Dark Secrets of the New Age: Satan's Plan for a One World Religion* (Westchester, Ill.: Good News Publishers, Crossway Books, 1987), p. 47.

134. "Lawmaker Asks Army to Prohibit Wiccan Rituals," *Austin American-Statesman*, 19 May 1999, A14; In the spring of 2001, religious-political conservatives objected to the possible inclusion of Wiccan and Islamic groups in charitable choice programs; The Federal Page, *Washington Post*, 25 September 2000, A19. According to the newspaper, the group posted the following statement on its website: "Our founders expected that Christianity — and no other religion — would receive support from the government as long as that support did not violate people's conscience and their right to worship. . . . They would have found utterly incredible the idea that all religions, including paganism, be treated with equal deference." The statement was subsequently withdrawn.

135. Paul Eshleman, *Showing God's Love to the World: The Jesus Film Project* (San Clemente, Cal.: Campus Crusade for Christ

International, May 2001). "More than 15 million people, most of whom have been highly resistant to the gospel and the powerful, evangelistic film, 'Jesus' — were in its path" (n.p.). After noting that the storm came ashore where a missionary and his two sons were killed by "Hindu militants," the letter goes on to describe the destruction and death caused by the storm. Eshleman writes, "For as yet, we have not heard of a single Christian who was killed. One island off the coast was totally destroyed, except for one village — a village of Christians" (n.p.). The author concludes by asking, "Was this storm judgment by God?" and opining that "millions of resistant — even hostile — people are now open to the gospel" (n.p.).

136. Ralph Reed, *Politically Incorrect* (Dallas: Word, 1994), p. 70.
137. Ibid., p. 48.
138. Amy Gutmann, "Why Should Schools Care About Civic Education?" in *Rediscovering the Democratic Purposes of Education*, edited by Lorraine M. McDonnell, P. Michael Timpane, and Roger Benjamin (Lawrence: University Press of Kansas, 2000), pp. 81-82.
139. Ibid., p. 82.
140. Yael Tamir, "Remember Amelek: Religious Hate Speech," in *Obligations of Citizenship and the Demands of Faith: Religious Accommodation in Pluralist Democracies*, edited by Nancy Rosenblum (Princeton, N.J.: Princeton University Press, 2000), p. 322.
141. Ibid., p. 323.
142. Ibid., quoting Kent Greenawalt, *Fighting Words: Individuals, Communities and Liberties of Speech* (Princeton, N.J.: Princeton University Press, 1995), p. 56.
143. Tamir, p. 323, quoting Greenawalt, p. 56.
144. Greenawalt, op. cit., p. 50.
145. Kent Greenawalt, "Free Speech in the United States and Canada," *Law and Contemporary Problems* (Winter 1992): 5-33.
146. Tamir, op. cit., p. 328, quoting Greenawalt, *Fighting Words*, p. 61.
147. *Planned Parenthood* v. *American Coalition of Life Activists*, 244 F.3d 1007 (9th Cir. 2001).

CHAPTER SIX

Democracy and Intolerance: Christian-School Curricula and Public Policy

Policy questions must be judged on two criteria: fairness and wisdom. The use of taxpayer funds, either through voucher programs (or, indeed, direct aid) or through tax policies to support religious education, requires policy makers and the public to determine whether such schemes meet these criteria. In the case of support for schools that use A Beka, Bob Jones, and Accelerated Christian Education textbooks, the issue of fairness involves the use of the tax code to force taxpayers to subsidize education institutions and programs that go beyond being merely contrary to their religious and political beliefs, but repeatedly denigrate many, if not most, taxpayers' religions and political values. The wisdom of this course forces us to confront the real possibility that increasing the numbers of students receiving an education based on the curricula described in this book poses a threat to our democratic institutions.

Coerced Support for Education that Denigrates Religious and Political Beliefs

Ironically, many religious-political conservatives, including those who also support vouchers and other programs that encourage attendance at religious schools, have deplored public school curricula and materials that allegedly denigrate religion. For example, Mel and Norma Gabler state that in public schools "[a]lmost without exception, any mention of the Bible or the Judeo-Christian ethic [is] degrading and hostile."[1] Robert Simonds of Citizens for Excellence in Education expresses opinions related to this issue most consistently and explicitly. He asks, "Shall we allow the unsaved, whether they are atheists or occultists, or the American Civil Liberties Union (ACLU), National Educational Association (NEA) or whomever, to decide on curriculum, what our children will be taught?"[2]

Many challenges brought against public school materials allege that they are blasphemous or "take the Lord's name in vain." Based on surveys conducted in 1963, 1966, 1973, 1977, and 1982, Burress listed 1,551 challenges to public school library books.[3] Of these, 76 (4.9%) could be categorized as related to the denigration of religion.[4] A 1997 analysis of challenges to public school materials based on annual reports published by the American Library Association and People for the American Way from 1983 to 1996 revealed that more than 7% and 9%, respectively, of religiously based challenges were brought on the grounds of religious denigration.[5] The Supreme Court itself has recognized; albeit in dicta, the issue of speech that denigrates religious beliefs. In *Marsh* v. *Chambers*, the Court upheld legislative prayers but opined that the result might have been different had the Nebraska legislative chaplain offered a prayer that "disparage[d] any other, faith or belief."[6]

Both conservatives and liberals argue that individuals should not be required to support organizations that express viewpoints with which they disagree. This was precisely the argument made by conservative activists in the 2000 Supreme Court decision related to funding of campus groups at the University of Wisconsin.[7] The issue in this case and others like it rests on the compelled speech doctrine that "protect[s] an individual's freedom of conscience by preventing the state from forcing an individual to become associated with an objectionable message."[8] This sentiment, whether it involves funding activities or associational messages, resonates with a significant number of citizens, from pacifists who object to funding the military to pro-choice activists opposing the use of student health fees for abortions or abortion counseling, from motorists objecting to sentiments emblazoned on license plates to nonbelievers objecting to tax-exempt status for churches. Indeed, no less a public figure than Lynn Cheney expressed this idea concisely when she protested public funding of the National Endowment for the Arts: "Government should not be funding those whose main interest is promoting an agenda."[9]

Perhaps even more ironic is the situation in which conservatives, especially those who support voucher programs, decry public funding for expressive activities that denigrate a particular religious faith. Speaking of artwork that offended many Christians, Tony Snow, a conservative columnist, wrote, "The government forces taxpayers to underwrite Andres Serrano's 'Piss Christ' — an 'artwork' consisting of a crucifix partially submerged in a beaker of urine."[10] More recently, Rudolph Giuliani, then mayor of New York and a strong voucher proponent, objected to art displayed at the Brooklyn Museum as blasphemous and anti-Catholic: "The fact is that I believe that public money should not be used to support desecration of religion or important national symbols."[11]

What I would hope that the reader recognizes is that there is a substantial difference between funding a museum in which religiously offensive art appears occasionally and requiring taxpayers to support schooling based on materials that are not merely offensive, but that systematically and pervasively denigrate and insult their religious beliefs. One distinction that can be drawn is that art museums frequently display works that treat religion in a reverential manner. The Christian school textbooks published or distributed by A Beka Books, Bob Jones University Press, and School of Tomorrow/Accelerated Christian Education do not accord the slightest element of respect to religious or political views with which their authors disagree. The reader must draw his or her own conclusions, but I believe asking a Roman Catholic, Hindu, Muslim, or Buddhist taxpayer to fund, whether directly or indirectly, the purchase of the textbooks I have described or the inculcation of children in the values the authors of these textbooks espouse is unconscionable. Justice Souter raised this issue in his dissent in *Zelman* v. *Simmons-Harris*.

> Not all taxpaying Protestant citizens, for example, will be content to underwrite the teaching of the Roman Catholic Church condemning the death penalty. Nor will all of America's Muslims acquiesce in paying for the endorsement of the religious Zionism taught in many religious Jewish schools, which combines "a nationalistic sentiment" in support of Israel with a "deeply religious" element. Nor will every secular taxpayer be content to support Muslim views on differential treatment of the sexes, or, for that matter, to fund the espousal of a wife's obligation of obedience to her husband, presumably taught in any schools adopting the articles of faith of the Southern Baptist Convention.[12]

Justice Souter may well have been thinking of a newspaper article in a spring 2002 *Washington Post* describing the anti-Jewish and anti-Christian materials used at a few Muslim schools in the United States.

Civic Education and Christian School Curricula

All education is balanced between exposing the student to the marketplace of ideas and inculcating the student in values of a particular group, whether that group consists of the family, the community, or the nation as a whole. This balance differs according to the level of education. In higher education, the mission of public colleges and universities and, to varying degrees, private institutions is to foster independence of thought by maximizing the exposure of the student to the marketplace of ideas and to a diversity of viewpoints. For the most part, inculcation in a particular set of values is minimized. In precollegiate education, the formation of a socially acceptable belief system assumes a greater prominence in the curriculum, and the inculcation of community values is fairly strongly supported by the courts.

Although parents have the right to select schools that use the curricular materials described in this book, that fact does not preclude a debate on the wisdom of encouraging parents to chose ideologically driven education. Nor does it mean that the implications of large numbers of parents choosing this type of education for their children should be ignored. Parents who choose conservative Protestant education for their children believe that public education is also ideologically driven and that the belief system that underlies public education is not only wrong but also detrimental to both their children's and the nation's well-being. The public and policy makers can and should ask whether the alternative system of Christian education for which they seek public approval and support is also ideologically driven in ways that run contrary to the best interests of a diverse, democratic society.

The privatization of American education is consistent with conservative ideology on two counts. First, it expresses the belief of religious-political conservatives that less government is superior to more government. Second, "privatization of education means that conservatives can establish their own schools in which their children will not have to learn anything that might be inconsistent with conservative morality and politics."[13] As we have seen, A Beka, Bob Jones, and School of Tomorrow/Accelerated Christian Education materials structure students' learning to avoid anything that might be inconsistent with conservative morality and politics. That parents have an unfettered right to educate their children in this manner is virtually beyond question. Set aside for the moment the arguments over whether the religious schools and other religious institutions (or in current parlance, "faith-based" institutions) should, under our Constitution, receive public funds. Set aside all the debates about the educational efficacy of public-to-private vouchers and private scholarship programs. The issue at hand is whether the government, using direct monetary subsidies, including vouchers, or indirect means (tax-advantaged education savings accounts, scholarship programs, or other tax incentives) should facilitate the education of children at schools that use the materials described in this book. The answer lies in our conception of civic education and takes us back to the most fundamental questions regarding the purposes of education.

Amy Gutmann, the Laurence S. Rockefeller University Professor of Politics at Princeton University, argues that "conscious social reproduction" is a sufficient reason to limit education that is repressive or discriminatory.[14] For me, the goal of "conscious social reproduction" encompasses both the knowledge and skills required for individuals and society to prosper in an economic and cultural sense and those habits of mind and the skills necessary to maintain the organizing principles of the society. For children, these attitudes and cognitive skills allow them to develop "the capacity to deliberate among alternative ways of personal and political life."[15] In a democratic society, these attributes and skills are those necessary to maintain a democratic form of government. Or as Gutmann puts it, "The democratic state is . . . committed to allocating its educational authority in such a way as to provide its members with an education adequate to participating in democratic politics, to choosing among (a limited range) of good lives, and to sharing in the several subcommunities, such as family, that impart identity to the lives of citizens."[16] Of the last of these, there can be little doubt that A Beka, Bob Jones, and School of Tomorrow materials facilitate students' ability to share in subcommunities, such as families, churches, and other social organizations. However, the problem lies in whether the type of "Christian education" exemplified in these texts facilitates students' ability to choose, as adults, among a range of good lives and to participate, as citizens, in democratic politics.

From this point forward I will use the term *Christian education* in its limited sense to denote specifically the forms of Christian schooling based on the textbooks and materials I have described.

The two questions of making life choices and participating fully as citizens in a democracy are related, and it is the repressive nature of Christian education that is at the heart of the conundrum. Gutmann sees "the principle of nonrepression [as] prevent[ing] the state or any group within it, from using education to restrict rational deliberation of competing conceptions of the good life and the good society" and defines "rational deliberation" as "consideration of different ways of life."[17] Little doubt should remain in the mind of the reader that Christian education, as described in this book, impedes a "consideration of different ways of life" and thus constrains the ability of those exposed to it for prolonged periods of time to choose ways of life different from those presented by the A Beka, Bob Jones, and School of Tomorrow/ Accelerated Christian Education authors. They make it clear that embracing "liberal" values is not acceptable and that living according to "liberal" values is contrary to God's will. Religious choices, too, are part of one's "good life." Students whose school experience is based in large part on the textbooks I have discussed are less free to choose a non-Christian faith — or, indeed, one that differs appreciably from conservative evangelical Protestantism — than are adults whose school experiences do not include reliance on materials that vigorously denigrate other faith traditions. But, of course, that is the purpose of these textbooks. Parents who select this type of school experience consciously intend to reduce the likelihood that their children will "fall into error" by choosing a "good life" that conflicts with their beliefs. In fact, living according to "liberal" values — for example, having a nontraditional relationship with one's spouse, being homosexual, supporting the United Nations, advocating a strong role for government, or choosing a different religion, such as becoming Roman Catholic, Muslim, or even Episcopalian — would lead to a life that could not be considered "good" by the limited Christian definition.

Most parents can empathize, at least in spirit if not in degree. Although parents may have differing views regarding the value of children freely choosing to live their own lives, parents do not rejoice when their child embraces what they consider a bad life. Even when parents fully support autonomy for young adults and adult children, if the parents consider the choice to be a bad one and the lifestyle to be harmful, then they are likely to oppose it just as conservative evangelical parents do. The difference is more of degree: the range of life choices that are labeled unacceptable and the strength with which this judgment is held. For example, "mainline" Presbyterian parents may be disappointed, perhaps even profoundly disappointed and disapproving, when their son or daughter becomes a Buddhist, but they may not find the child's choice to be "evil." For many, if not virtually all, conservative Protestants, such a choice would mean the "eternal damnation" of their child. Parents who believe in an egalitarian marriage may not find their child's decision to establish a marriage based on traditional gender roles a comfortable one and may believe the child has made a "wrong" decision, but the parent is unlikely to view the child's lifestyle as deeply immoral, sinful, or evil. However, from a perspective of allowing people to define and choose among a number of "good lives," a Christian education is inherently repressive and mitigates against what Gutmann terms "deliberative freedom."[18]

Christian education affects far more than the ability of individuals to freely choose among possible good lives. It is fundamentally contrary to reproduction of democratic governments because it impedes students' ability, as adults, to deliberate critically among "a range of . . . the good societies."[19] And this, in turn, affects students' ability to "participat[e] in democratic politics."[20] The ability to participate in democratic politics requires that citizens be able to conduct a discourse based on reason. Such discourse admits that opposing viewpoints and conceptions of the good society may be legitimate. "I may think you are wrong, but I will give your opinion a fair hearing." If, as Gutmann opines, the "foundations for rational deliberation of differing ways of life" rest on citizens having "characters traits, such as religious tolerance and mutual respect for persons" that make shared sovereignty possible, then Christian education is inimical to democratic civil discourse.[21]

Grudging, angry tolerance in which those who hold differing religious beliefs are viewed as both contemptible and threatening is a shaky foundation on which to build a diverse society. Tolerance is fundamental to democracy — all the more so as the population becomes increasingly diverse. History teaches us that religion is among the most volatile human values; and democracy requires compromise, civil discourse, and deliberation based on a relatively full range of options. If a group of citizens, especially a large group of citizens, cannot see any merit whatsoever in the positions taken by their opponents, then they may fail to consider viable options and their resentment over compromises may generate profound fractures in the polity. Because students who truly absorb the lessons taught by the authors of Christian school textbooks would be less able to respect those who hold different social, political, and religious views, their ability to engage in civil discourse is likely to be seriously impaired. Can students who are taught that liberal = socialist = communist = evolutionist = sinner and heretic engage in a dialogue that allows for the fact that a liberal solution or policy might have merit, might actually be the best choice?

In these textbooks, the message that political beliefs and affiliation are related to a person's standing in the eyes of God is particularly troubling. Can a person who has absorbed the lesson that Hindus are slothful or dirty because of their religion truly listen to a fellow citizen who is Hindu? Can a person who believes that Catholics are followers of a distorted, perverted, and false religion be able to engage in an open and meaningful dialogue with their fellow citizens who are Roman Catholics? Can a person who believes that "liberal" is just another word for "socialist" or "Communist" and that these political systems would be the destruction of their most cherished beliefs — or are inspired by Satan — be able to consider "liberal" solutions to problems? This issue was of particular concern to Justices Stevens, Souter, and Breyer in their dissenting opinions in *Zelman* v. *Simmons-Harris*.[22]

A further danger to the ability of citizens to engage in rational civic discourse lies in the texts' failure to teach students to distinguish between fact and opinion. As I noted in Chapter One, these materials contain vast amounts of purely factual material; but the authors continually interpose persuasive commentary. As citizens, "we bear the burden of distinguishing between legitimate and spurious moral distinctions."[23] That skill requires us to be able to distinguish fact from opinion. The root of critical thinking is the ability to sort out factual material from persuasive arguments. When young people are continually exposed to books that fail to make any distinction between fact and opinion, it seems logical to assume that, as adults, their ability to recognize the difference would be seriously impaired. These are not curricula that present only factual material (this in itself would compromise the ability to make such judgments); but curricula where opinion and facts are presented as a unified whole, constantly mixed together without any distinction being made between the two.

A final danger posed by the use of these materials lies in the influence they may have on young people who are emotionally unstable. Proponents of Christian education will no doubt take great offense at this contention, and perhaps they are justified. There may be those who take this statement out of context to support an ideological position.[24] Critics of secular education in today's public schools have argued that they fail to teach moral values, which may have a deleterious effect on students exposed to public school curricula. And by their lights, it does. Nevertheless, I would be remiss if I did not raise the possibility that prolonged exposure to a curriculum dominated by books that foster resentment toward government and strong and unequivocal condemnation of people with different political, social, and religious beliefs may well have a deeply corrosive effect on young people who are both impressionable and emotionally unstable. Conservatives have long argued that exposure to public school curricula, including books found in school libraries, and to vulgarity and violence in the media can harm children and adolescents. Taking this assertion as valid, it seems just as likely that prolonged exposure to school textbooks that encourage resentment and anger toward the government in general and governmental programs and policies and that denigrate others based on their religious, political, and social values or affiliations might well — unintentionally, to be sure — cause profound alienation and disaffection in a number of young people. In addition, it is not unreasonable to suppose that some of those young people, when they become adults, might engage in antisocial behavior. No doubt the vast majority of children who use A Beka, Bob

Jones, and Accelerated Christian Education materials will go on to lead lives of moral rectitude (though I would guess that the majority will find themselves most comfortable with conservative ideas) and become law-abiding citizens. Nevertheless, the Christian Identity movement and other right-wing organizations differ from such "mainstream" religious-political and social conservatives as Phyllis Schlafly, James Dobson, Pat Robertson, Jerry Falwell, and Gary Bauer more in the degree with which they hold their core beliefs than in the actual nature of their ideology.[25]

The Christian school curricula that I have examined pose a risk that a higher percentage of young people who are exposed to it for a long time will fall prey to conspiratorial thinking or engage in antisocial and criminal acts than will those who are exposed to the curricula used in public, secular private, or parochial schools or in other religious schools. I am not saying that the proportion of students, other factors being equal, who engage in such acts as adults is higher when those children have received a Christian education than it is for youngsters who attended public schools. Indeed, my sense of the matter is that students who attend Christian schools are much less likely to become criminals than are those in the general population or public school attendees. What I am saying is that Christian school curricula based on A Beka, Bob Jones, and School of Tomorrow/Accelerated Christian Education materials may, when compared with public school curricula, be more likely to lead emotionally unstable young people to identify with and join Christian Identity and militia-type movements, including pro-life movements that espouse violence toward abortion clinics and providers.

Should schools that use materials from A Beka, Bob Jones, and Accelerated Christian Education be permitted to exist? Clearly, under our constitutional system they have that right. This is not the real question. Nor is the question whether parents should be permitted to select this type of education for their children. One of the most deeply cherished values in American society, and in any society that considers itself to be free, is the right to rear one's children free from state interference; and this right cannot be separated from the right to communicate the beliefs of the parents to their children. In *Pierce* v. *Society of Sisters*, the Supreme Court upheld the right of parents to delegate that right to others.[26] In a free society, parents have this right, though it is not entirely unfettered. Any society has a deep interest in the education of its young people. When I go to the dentist, I sincerely hope that the technician had a secure educational foundation for his or her training. When I go to the polling booth, I hope that the other voters have given serious consideration to all the ramifications of the choices before us. I hope that my fellow Americans respect my most cherished beliefs, even when they disagree with them. And this public interest in the education of its future citizens is reflected in both policy and law.

Rather, the question is whether we as a society should enact laws and policies that encourage the proliferation of schools that use A Beka, Bob Jones, School of Tomorrow/Accelerated Christian Education, and similar curricula. Policy makers and, at some juncture, the public at large must confront the issue that the exposure of school children to these materials might be detrimental to the development of civic virtue in our future citizens. That they have not done so reflects a lack of knowledge about the nature of Christian education and the implications of fostering a system of education that is as threatening to democracy as its adherents see public education is threatening to the moral health of their children and the nation.

Setting aside issues related to church-state separation, there is evidence that the courts might take a less benign view of the various programs to funnel public support to religious schools through tax-advantaged programs or vouchers if they had before them a more complete record regarding the nature of Christian school curricula. In *Bob Jones University* v. *United States*, the Supreme Court denied the university tax-exempt status on the ground that the university's racially discriminatory admissions policy was contrary to the public interest.[27] The Court found that the university's status as a 501(c)(3) charitable institution should be revoked because its policies were "not in harmony with the public interest [and were] at odds with the common community conscience."[28] Even though the policies might spring from sincere religious beliefs, they were not "'beneficial and stabilizing influences on community life' [and should not] be encouraged by having all taxpayers share in their support by way of special tax status."[29] It can be argued that school curricula that encourage prejudice against other Americans on the basis of their religion also is neither a beneficial nor stabilizing community influence and should not be supported by taxpayers. A court might well conclude, as the Court did in *Marsh* when addressing the issue of legislative prayers, that vouchers are unconstitutional because the curriculum of some participating schools "disparages . . . other faith[s] or belief[s]."

Notes

1. *Victims of Censorship* (Longview, Texas: Educational Research Analysts, n.d.), p. 4.
2. Robert Simonds, *President's Report* (Costa Mesa, Calif.: National Association of Christian Educators/Citizens for Excellence in Education, October 1996), p. 3.
3. Lee Burress, *Battle of the Books: Literary Censorship in the Public Schools, 1950-1985* (Metuchen, N.J.: Scarecrow, 1989).
4. Frances R.A. Paterson, *Legally Related Religious Challenges to Public School Materials, Curricula, and Instructional Activities: The "Impressions" Challenges, 1986-1994* (Ann Arbor, Mich: University Microfilms, 1997), p. 213.
5. Ibid., pp. 213-15.
6. *Marsh* v. *Chambers*, 463 U.S. 783, 794 (1983).
7. Jon G. Furlow, "The Price of Free Speech: *Regents* v. *Southworth*," *Wisconsin Lawyer* (June 2000): 14-18; Meredith R. Miller, "*Southworth* v. *Grebe*: The Conservative Utilization of 'Negative' First Amendment Rights to Attack Diversity of Thought at Public Universities," *Brooklyn Law Review* (Spring 1999): 529-83.
8. Furlow, op. cit., p. 17.
9. Tom Brazaitis, "Congress to Decide Fate of Arts Funding," (Cleveland) *Plain Dealer*, 12 February 1995, p. 18A.

10. Tony Snow, "Religion Ruled Out of Public Life," *St. Louis Post-Dispatch*, 24 December 1997, p. B7.

11. Robert Polner, "News," *Newsday*, 25 September 1999, p. A8.

12. *Zelman* v. *Simmons-Harris*, 122 S.Ct. 2460, 2501 (2002) (5-4 decision) (Souter, J., dissenting). According to Ali Al-Ahmed, "whose Virginia-based Saudi Institute promotes religious tolerance in Saudi Arabia," textbooks used at the Islamic Saudi Academy in suburban Virginia, a school with approximately 1,300 students and financed by the Saudi Arabian government, "promote hatred of non-Muslims and Shiite Muslims. The 11th-grade textbook, for example, says one sign of the Day of Judgment will be that Muslims will fight and kill Jews, who will hide behind trees that say: 'Oh Muslim, Oh servant of God, here is a Jew hiding behind me. Come here and kill him'." Valerie Strauss and Emily Wax, "Where Two Worlds Collide: Muslim Schools Face Tension of Islamic, U.S. Views," *Washington Post*, 25 February 2002, p. A1. A subsequent *Newsday* article pointed out that vouchers might be used at Islamic schools described in the *Post* article. Carol R. Richards, "States Shouldn't Subsidize Religious Schools," *Newsday*, 10 March 2002, p. B8.

13. George Lakoff, *Moral Politics: What Conservatives Know That Liberals Don't* (Chicago: University of Chicago Press, 1996), pp. 230-31.

14. Amy Gutmann, *Democratic Education* (Princeton, N.J.: Princeton University Press, 1987).

15. Ibid., p. 40.

16. Ibid., p. 42.

17. Ibid., p. 44.

18. Ibid., p. 46.

19. Ibid., p. 44.

20. Ibid., p. 42.

21. Ibid., p. 44.

22. "Whenever we remove a brick from the wall that was designed to separate religion and government, we increase the risk of religious strife and weaken the foundation of our democracy." *Zelman* v. *Simmons-Harris*, 122 S.Ct. 2460, 2485 (2002) (5-4 decision) (Stevens, J., dissenting). Justice Souter noted that a major purpose behind the Establishment Clause was the avoidance of social con-

flict. Ibid., p. 2501 (Souter, J., dissenting). Justice Breyer wrote, "I fear that [vouchers will create] a form of religiously based conflict potentially harmful to the nation's social fabric." Ibid., p. 2508 (Breyer, J., dissenting).

23. Ibid., p. 41.

24. "Berliner has many allies in spreading such apocalyptic messages. For example, Frances Paterson . . . in the Department of Educational Leadership at Valdosta State University in Georgia, concluded an analysis of Christian school history and civics textbooks by sounding this alarm: 'As we debate the wisdom of various proposals to privatize all or part of American education, we should consider whether such training might increase the Balkanization of our society and lower the quality of public discourse by encouraging young people to develop a value system that is based on an us-versus-them world view'." Howard Fuller and Kaleem Caire, "Lies and Distortions: The Campaign Against School Vouchers" (Milwaukee: Institute for the Transformation of Learning, Marquette University, 2001), 22-23, quoting Frances R.A. Paterson, "Building a Conservative Base: Teaching History and Civics in Voucher-Supported Schools," *Phi Delta Kappan* (October 2000). Fuller and Caire do not address the characteristics of the textbooks I describe in the article. Interestingly, the authors, who are professors at a Roman Catholic university, make no reference to an article on the anti-Catholic bias in Christian school textbooks that was cited in the *Kappan* article.

25. For a discussion of the complex interrelationship between conservative and hard-right organizations, see Chip Berlot and Matthew N. Lyons, *Right-Wing Populism in America: Too Close for Comfort* (New York: Guildford Press, 2000), pp. 175-352.

26. 268 U.S. 510, 522 (1925).

27. *Bob Jones University* v. *United States*, 461 U.S. 574 (1983).

28. Ibid., p. 591.

29. Ibid., p. 595, quoting *Walz* v. *Tax Comm'n*, 397 U.S. 664, 673 (1970).

BIBLIOGRAPHY

Textbooks Examined

Note: School of Tomorrow publications are published by School of Tomorrow, Accelerated Christian Education, and Reform Publications.

The Age of Exploration. Self-Pac® of Basic Education (#104). Rev. 1997. Reform Publications, 1974.

Age of Reform, 1865-1900. Self-Pac® of Basic Education (#117). Rev. 1996. Reform Publications, 1974.

American Origins: The Age of Discovery and Explorations. Self-Pac® of Basic Education (#109). Rev. 1995. Reform Publications, 1974.

The American Republic for Christian Schools. Teachers Edition. Greenville, S.C.: Bob Jones University Press, 1988.

Anderson, Jan, and Hicks, Laurel. *Introduction to English Literature.* 2nd ed. Pensacola, Fla.: A Beka, 1996.

Approaching the Twenty-First Century. Self-Pac® of Basic Education (#108). Rev. 1997. Reform Publications, 1996.

Bowen, William R.; Thompson, George T.; Lowman, Michael R.; and Cochran, George C. *American Government in Christian Perspective.* 2nd. ed. Pensacola, Fla.: A Beka, 1997.

Colonial Period. Self-Pac® of Basic Education (#110). Rev. 1995. Reform Publications, 1974.

Combee, Jerry H. *History of the World in Christian Perspective.* Teacher Edition. 3rd ed. Pensacola, Fla.: A Beka, 1995.

Doors of Opportunity: Nineteenth Century America. Teacher's Edition. Heritage Studies for Christian Schools 4. Greenville, S.C.: Bob Jones University Press, 1997.

Early Middle Ages. Self-Pac® of Basic Education (#101). Rev. 1995. Reform Publications, 1974.

Eastern Hemisphere Nations. Heritage Studies for Christian Schools 6. Greenville, S.C.: Bob Jones University Press, 1986.

English IV-3. (#1135). Rev. 1995. Accelerated Christian Education, 1993.

Fisher, David A. *World History for Christian Schools.* Teacher's Edition. 2nd ed. Greenville, S.C.: Bob Jones University Press, 1994.

Grussendorf, Kurt A.; Lowman, Michael R.; and Ashbaugh, Brian S. *America: Land That I Love.* Teacher Edition. Pensacola, Fla.: A Beka, 1994.

The History of Our United States. Teacher Edition. Pensacola, Fla.: A Beka, 1998.

Horton, Ronald A. *British Literature for Christian Schools.* Teacher's Edition. Greenville, S.C.: Bob Jones University Press, 1997.

Keesee, Timothy. *American Government for Christian Schools.* Teacher's Edition. Greenville, S.C.: Bob Jones University Press, 1998.

Keesee, Timothy, and Sidwell, Mark. *United States History for Christian Schools.* Teacher's Edition. 2nd ed. Pensacola, Fla.: A Beka, 1991.

Lowman, Michael; Thompson, George; and Grussendorf, Kurt. *United States History in Christian Perspective: Heritage of Freedom.* 2nd ed. Pensacola, Fla.: A Beka, 1996.

The Making of Modern Europe. Self-Pac® of Basic Education (#105). Reform Publications, 1974.

Old World History and Geography. Teacher Edition. Pensacola, Fla.: A Beka, 1991.

The Post-World War II Period. Self-Pac® of Basic Education (#120). School of Tomorrow, 1998.

Renaissance and Reformation. Self-Pac® of Basic Education (#103). Reform Publications, 1974.

Rising Sectionalism. Self-Pac® of Basic Education (#113). School of Tomorrow, 1974.

Social Studies. Self-Pac® of Basic Education (#107). Rev. 1997. Reform Publications, 1974.

Social Studies 1041. Rev. 1998. Accelerated Christian Education, 1981.

Social Studies 1043. Rev. 1998. Accelerated Christian Education, 1981.

Social Studies 1044. Rev. 1998. Accelerated Christian Education, 1981.

Social Studies 1045. Rev. 1998. Accelerated Christian Education, 1981.

Social Studies 1046. Rev. 1998. Accelerated Christian Education, 1981.

Social Studies 1047. Rev. 1998. Accelerated Christian Education, 1981.

Social Studies 1050. Accelerated Christian Education, 1981.

Social Studies 1066. Rev. 1998. Accelerated Christian Education, 1982.

Social Studies 1085. Rev. 1998. Accelerated Christian Education, 1990.

Social Studies 1088. Rev. 1998. Accelerated Christian Education, 1990.

Social Studies 1091. Rev. 1998. Accelerated Christian Education, 1990.

Social Studies 1093. Rev. 1998. Accelerated Christian Education, 1990.

Social Studies 1094. Rev. 1998. Accelerated Christian Education, 1990.

Social Studies 1095. Rev. 1998. Accelerated Christian Education, 1990.

Social Studies 1096. Rev. 1998. Accelerated Christian Education, 1990.

Social Studies, U.S. Civics-2 (#1134). School of Tomorrow, 1998.

Social Studies, U.S. Civics-4 (#1136). School of Tomorrow, 1997.

St. John, Raymond A. *American Literature for Christian Schools*. Teacher's Edition. Greenville, S.C.: Bob Jones University Press, 1994.

Teacher's Resource Guide to Current Events for Christian Schools, 1998-1999. Greenville, S.C.: Bob Jones University Press, 1998.

Thompson, George, and Combee, Jerry. *World History and Cultures in Christian Perspective*. 2nd ed. Pensacola, Fla.: A Beka, 1997.

The Turn of the Century, 1890-1914. Self-Pac® of Basic Education (#118). Rev. 1996. Reform Publications, 1998.

Westward Expansion. Self-Pac® of Basic Education (#115). Rev. 1995. Reform Publications, 1974.

World Geography-3. Social Studies (#1099). Rev. 1996. Accelerated Christian Education, 1994.

World Geography-10. Social Studies (#1106). Rev. 1998. Accelerated Christian Education, 1994.

World History Between 1850 and 1950. Self-Pac® of Basic Education (#106). Rev. 1995. Reform Publications, 1974.

World Studies for Christian Schools. Teacher's Edition, Greenville, S.C.: Bob Jones University Press, 1993.

Relevant Court Cases

Bob Jones University v. United States, 461 U.S. 2017 (1983).

Brown v. Board of Educ., 347 U.S. 483 (1954).

Brown v. Board of Educ. II, 349 U.S. 294 (1955).

Chaplinsky v. New Hampshire, 315 U.S. 568 (1942).

Church of the Holy Trinity v. United States, 143 U.S. 457 (1892).

Church of the Lukumi Babalu Aye v. Hialeah, 508 U.S. 520 (1993).

Cohen v. California, 403 U.S. 15 (1971).

Dennis v. United States, 341 U.S. 494 (1951).

Dred Scott v. Sandford, 60 U.S. 393 (1857).

Employment Div. v. Smith, 494 U.S. 872 (1990).

Engel v. Vitale, 370 U.S. 421 (1962).

Furman v. Georgia, 408 U.S. 238 (1972).

Trustees of Dartmouth College v. Woodward, 17 U.S. 518 (1819).
United States v. Butler, 297 U.S. 1 (1936).
Vidal v. Girard's Executors, 43 U.S. 127 (1844).
West Virginia Bd. of Educ. v. Barnette, 319 U.S. 624 (1943).
Zelman v. Simmons-Harris, 122 S.Ct. 2460 (2002).

Resources

Altbach, Phillip G.; Kelly, Gail P.; Petrie, Hugh G.; and Weis, Lois, eds.
    Textbooks in American Society: Politics, Policy, and Pedagogy.
    Albany: State University of New York Press, 1991.
Apple, Michael W., and Christian-Smith, Linda K. *The Politics of the
    Textbook.* New York: Routledge, 1991.
Berliner, David C. "Educational Psychology Meets the Christian Right:
    Differing Views of Children, Schooling, Teaching, and Learning."
    Teachers College Record 98 (Spring 1997): 381-415.
Berliner, David C., and Biddle, Bruce J. *The Manufactured Crisis:
    Myths, Fraud, and the Attacks on America's Public Schools.* Read-
    ing, Mass.: Addison-Wesley, 1995.
Berlot, Chip, and Lyons, Matthew N. *Right-Wing Populism in America:
    Too Close for Comfort.* New York: Guildford, 2000.
"A Biblical Approach to Objective Elements in Literature." *Home
    School Helper*, Bob Jones University Press (October 2002): 6.
Broughman, Stephen P., and Colaciello, Lenore A. *Private School
    Universe Survey, 1995-1996.* Washington, D.C.: United States De-
    partment of Education, National Center for Educational Statistics,
    1998. http://nces.ed.gov/pubs/98229.pdf
Broughman, Stephen P., and Colaciello, Lenore A. *Private School
    Universe Survey, 1997-1998.* Washington, D.C.: United States De-
    partment of Education, National Center for Educational Statistics,
    1999. http://nces.ed.gov/pubs99/1999319.pdf
Burress, Lee. *Battle of the Books: Literary Censorship in the Public
    Schools, 1950-1985.* Metuchen, N.J.: Scarecrow, 1989.
Carper, James C., and Hunt, Thomas C., eds. *Religious Schooling in
    America.* Birmingham, Ala.: Religious Education Press, 1984.
Chick, Jack T. *Are Roman Catholics Christians?* Ontario, Cal.: Chick
    Publications, 1985. http://www.chick.com/reading/tracts/0071/
    0071_01.asp

Chick, Jack T. *Last Rites*. Pamphlet. Ontario, Cal.: Chick Publications, 1994. http://www.chick.com/catalog/tractlist.asp

Chick, Jack T. *Why Is Mary Crying?* Pamphlet. Ontario, Cal.: Chick Publications, 1987. http://www.chick.com/reading/tracts/0040/0040_01.asp

Cloud, David C. *Fundamentalism, Modernism, and New-Evangelicalism, Part II*. Port Huron, Mich.: Fundamental Baptist Information Service/Way of Life Literature, 1999. http://www.camano.net/dcloud/fbns/fundamen2.htm

Cookson, Peter W., Jr. *School Choice: The Struggle for the Soul of American Education*. New Haven, Conn.: Yale University Press, 1994.

Cumbey, Constance E. *The Hidden Dangers of the Rainbow: The New Age Movement and Our Coming Age of Barbarism*. Rev. ed. Lafayette, La.: Huntington House, 1983.

Davis, Wanda Jean. *The Alternative Educational Systems of Two Fundamentalist Christian School Publishers*. Ann Arbor, Mich.: University Microfilms, 1990.

"Dumbing Down and Developing Diversity." *Phyllis Schlafly Report* (March 2001): 1.

Durham, Martin. *The Christian Right, the Far Right, and the Boundaries of American Conservatism*. Manchester, England, and New York: Manchester University Press, 2000.

Elson, Ruth Miller. *Guardians of Tradition: American Schoolbooks of the Nineteenth Century*. Lincoln: University of Nebraska Press, 1964.

Eshleman, Paul. *Showing God's Love to the World: The Jesus Film Project*. San Clemente, Cal.: Campus Crusade for Christ International, May 2001.

"Faith-Based Funding Backed, but Church-State Doubts Abound." Online. Pew Research Center, n.d. [cited 21 May 2001]. http://people-press.org/reports/display.php3?PageID=112

Falwell, Jerry. *America Can Be Saved*. Murfreesboro, Tenn.: Sword of the Lord, 1979.

Falwell, Jerry. *Listen, America!* Garden City, N.Y.: Doubleday, 1980.

Fleming, Dan B., and Hunt, Thomas C. "The World as Seen by Students in Accelerated Christian Education Schools." *Phi Delta Kappan* 66 (March 1987): 518-23.

Fraser, James W. *Between Church and State: Religion and Public Education in a Multicultural America*. New York: St. Martin's, Griffin, 1999.

Fuller, Bruce; Elmore, Richard F.; and Orfield, Gary, eds. *Who Chooses? Who Loses? Culture, Institutions, and the Unequal Effects of School Choice*. New York: Teachers College Press, 1996.

Fuller, Howard, and Caire, Kaleem. *Lies and Distortions: The Campaign Against School Vouchers*. Milwaukee: Institute for the Transformation of Learning, Marquette University, 2001. http://www.schoolchoiceinfo.org/hot_topic/pdf/10.pdf

Furlow, Jon G. "The Price of Free Speech: *Regents* v. *Southworth*." *Wisconsin Lawyer* 73 (June 2000): 14-18.

Gabler, Mel, and Gabler, Norma. *What Are They Teaching Our Children?* Wheaton, Ill.: Victor, 1986.

Gaddy, Barbara. B.; Hall, T. William; and Marzano, Robert J. *School Wars: Resolving Our Conflicts over Religion and Values*. San Francisco: Jossey-Bass, 1996.

Gehring, John. "Voucher Battles Head to State Capitals." *Education Week*, 10 July 2002, pp. 1, 24, 25.

Greenawalt, Kent. "Free Speech in the United States and Canada." *Law and Contemporary Problems* 55 (Winter 1992): 5-33.

Groothuis, Douglas R. *Unmasking the New Age*. Downers Grove, Ill.: InterVarsity, 1986.

Gutmann, Amy. *Democratic Education*. Princeton: Princeton University Press, 1987.

Gutmann, Amy. "Why Should Schools Care About Civic Education?" In *Rediscovering the Democratic Purposes of Education*, edited by Lorraine M. McDonnell, P. Michael Timpane, and Roger Benjamin. Lawrence: University Press of Kansas, 2000.

Hardy, Richard J. *Government in America*. Boston: Houghton Mifflin, 1993.

Henig, Jeffrey R. *Rethinking School Choice: Limits of the Market Metaphor*. Princeton, N.J.: Princeton University Press, 1994.

Higham, John. *Strangers in the Land: Patterns of American Nativisim, 1860-1925*. New Brunswick, N.J.: Rutgers University Press, 1992.

Hunter, James Davison. *Culture Wars: The Struggle to Define America*. New York: HarperCollins, 1991.

Kemerer, Frank R. "The Constitutionality of School Vouchers." *West's Education Law Reporter* 101 (August 1995): 17-36.

Knoebel, Dale T. *America for the Americans: The Nativist Movement in the United States.* New York: Simon and Schuster, Macmillan, 1996.

LaHaye, Tim. *The Battle for the Public Schools: Humanism's Threat to Our Children.* Old Tappan, N.J.: F.H. Revell, 1983.

Lakoff, George. *Moral Politics: What Conservatives Know that Liberals Don't.* Chicago: University of Chicago Press, 1996.

Ledell, Marjorie, and Arnsparger, Arleen. *How to Deal with Community Criticism of School Change.* Alexandria, Va: Association for Supervision and Curriculum Development, 1993.

Lubet, Steven. "The Ten Commandments in Alabama." *Constitutional Commentary* 15 (Fall 1998): 471-78.

Marrs, Texe. *Dark Secrets of the New Age: Satan's Plan for a One World Religion.* Westchester, Ill.: Good News Publishers, Crossway Books, 1987.

Mead, Julie F. "The Milwaukee Parental Choice Program: A Experiment Challenged." In *25 Years After Yoder: Educational Alternatives. Education Law Association Annual Conference.* Seattle: Education Law Association, 1997.

Mead, Sidney E. *The Lively Experiment: The Shaping of Christianity in America.* New York: Harper & Row, 1963.

Menendez, Albert J. *Visions of Reality: What Fundamentalist Schools Teach.* Buffalo, N.Y.: Prometheus, 1993.

Miller, Meredith R. "*Southworth* v. *Grebe*: The Conservative Utilization of 'Negative' First Amendment Rights to Attack Diversity of Thought at Public Universities." *Brooklyn Law Review* 65 (Spring 1999): 529-83.

Morris, Barbara M. *Change Agents in the Schools.* Elliot City, Md.: Barbara Morris Report, 1979.

National Center for Educational Statistics. *Private School Universe Survey, 1993-1994.* Washington, D.C.: U.S. Department of Education, National Center for Educational Statistics, 1996. http://nces.ed.gov/pubs/96143.pdf

Ornstein, Alan C., and Hunkins, Francis P. *Curriculum: Foundations, Principles, and Issues.* 3rd ed. Boston: Allyn and Bacon, 1998.

Parsons, Paul F. *Inside America's Christian Schools.* Macon, Ga.: Mercer University Press, 1987.

Paterson, Frances R.A. *Legally Related Religious Challenges to Public School Materials, Curricula, and Instructional Activities: The*

"Impressions" Challenges, 1986-1994. Ann Arbor, Mich: University Microfilms, 1997.

Peshkin, Alan. *God's Choice: The Total World of a Fundamentalist Christian School.* Chicago: University of Chicago Press, 1986.

Peterson, Paul E., and Hassel, Bryan C. *Learning from School Choice.* Washington, D.C.: Brookings Institution, 1998.

Provenzo, Eugene F., Jr. *Religious Fundamentalism and American Education: The Battle for the Public Schools.* Albany: State University of New York Press, 1990.

Reed, Ralph. *Politically Incorrect.* Dallas: Word, 1994.

Robertson, Pat. "The New Millennium." In *The Collected Works of Pat Robertson: The New Millennium, The New World Order, The Secret Kingdom.* New York: Inspirational Press, 1994.

Rose, Susan D. *Keeping Them Out of the Hands of Satan: Evangelical Schooling in America.* New York: Routledge, 1988.

Simonds, Robert. *President's Report.* Costa Mesa, Cal.: National Association of Christian Educators/Citizens for Excellence in Education, October 1996.

Tamir, Yael. "Remember Amelek: Religious Hate Speech." In *Obligations of Citizenship and the Demands of Faith: Religious Accommodation in Pluralist Democracies,* edited by Nancy Rosenblum. Princeton, N.J.: Princeton University Press, 2000.

Van Geel, Tyll, and Boyd, William. "Vouchers and the Entanglement of Church and State." *Education Week,* 4 September 2002, pp. 46-49.

Witte, John F. "The Milwaukee Voucher Experiment" *Educational Evaluation and Policy Review* 20 (Winter 1998): 229-51.

ABOUT THE AUTHOR

Frances Paterson was born in Richmond, Surrey, England. After her family immigrated to the United States, she attended school in New York and North Carolina. She attended East Mecklenburg High School in Charlotte, North Carolina, starting college at the end of her junior year. Paterson graduated from Queens College with a degree in economics at the age of 20. She received her fifth-year teaching certificate  in secondary social studies education from Davidson College in North Carolina.

After teaching junior high school in the Lancaster (South Carolina) City Schools, Paterson received her master's degree in education with a specialization in school librarianship from Winthrop College. Later she served as media specialist at Dilworth Elementary School in the Charlotte-Mecklenburg public schools.

Paterson received a law degree and a doctorate in educational administration from the University of Oklahoma. Currently, she teaches courses in school law, higher education law, special education law, and professional ethics for educators at Valdosta State University in Georgia, where she is an associate professor of educational leadership. She is the author of numerous articles on religion and church and state issues in American education.